Ask the Master

Also by Harold Klemp:

The Book of ECK Parables, Volume 1
The Book of ECK Parables, Volume 2
The Book of ECK Parables, Volume 3
Child in the Wilderness
The Living Word
Soul Travelers of the Far Country
The Spiritual Exercises of ECK
The Temple of ECK
The Wind of Change

The Mahanta Transcripts Series

Journey of Soul, Book 1
How to Find God, Book 2
The Secret Teachings, Book 3
The Golden Heart, Book 4
Cloak of Consciousness, Book 5
Unlocking the Puzzle Box, Book 6
The Eternal Dreamer, Book 7
The Dream Master, Book 8

MAHANTA

This book has been authored by and published under the supervision of the Living ECK Master, Sri Harold Klemp. It is the Word of ECK.

Ask the Master

Book 1

Harold Klemp

ECKANKAR
Minneapolis, MN

Printed in U.S.A.

Compiled by Sharon Douse and Mary Carroll Moore
Edited by Joan Klemp and Anthony Moore

Cover design by Lois Stanfield
Cover photo by Luanne Lawton
Cover photo hand-colored by Peg Bonner
Text illustrations by Signy Cohen

Second Printing—1994

Publisher's Cataloging in Publication
(Prepared by Quality Books Inc.)
Klemp, Harold.
    Ask the master / Harold Klemp.
     p. cm. — (Ask the master ; bk. 1)
    Preassigned LCCN: 93-70681.
    ISBN 1-57043-012-8
    1. Eckankar I. Title. II. Series: Klemp, Harold. Ask the master ; bk. 1
BP605.E3K554 1994   299'.93
                           QBI93-1188

Life is acknowledged to be a stormy sea. Yet so often when the boat rocks we fly into a panic, as if a boat shouldn't rock in a storm.

The storms of life separate the cosmic sailors from the meek landlubbers. It is the Way of ECK. Look to the Light and Sound of God within you, and you will always sail the cosmic sea of ECK.

—Sri Harold Klemp

Contents

Introduction xi

1. Dreams 1
   Are Dreams Real? • Start Remembering Your Dreams
   • Open Your Spiritual Eye • Increased Dream Aware-
   ness • When You Dream about the ECK Masters •
   Invite the Mahanta Along • Dreams within Dreams •
   Lucid Dreaming • Jumping through Experiences • Is
   It Real, or Is It a Symbol? • Protect Yourself from
   Nightmares • Dream Tests • Your Dream Sword • Fear
   of Death in Dreams • Controlling Your Life • Falling
   Sensations • Dreams Are Subtle • Sharing Dreams •
   Soul's Freedom • Familiar Dream Worlds • Preparing
   for Your Future • Dreams about Ancient Times • Are
   You Ready to Begin? • Learning New Laws • Serving
   Others in Dreams • The Gentle Way of Dreaming •
   Three Steps for Better Dreaming

2. Spiritual Protection 29
   How Are ECKists Protected? • Domes of Energy •
   Personal Protection • Protection from Others • Free-
   dom from Suffering • Shifting Your Attention • Protec-
   tion after Death • Express Lane • Ways to Heal Yourself
   • Protection with HU • Becoming a Happier Person •
   Are You Trapped by Time? • How HU Can Heal You •
   What the ECK Masters Want for You

3. Solving Problems 41
   Why Do Troubles Come? • Be Kinder to Yourself • Are
   You Mixing Two Paths? • Take Care of Yourself First
   • Why Troubles Equal Unfoldment • Attitudes Create
   Your World • Rising from Failure • Lack of Harmony

with Others • How Problems Change as You Grow • Doing Things That Frighten Us • Soul's Love for God • The Road to God

4. **Past Lives and the ECK-Vidya** 55

Past-Life Study Tips • How to Unwind Your Karma • Time Twins • Can You See Past Lives? • Friends from the Past • Reading the ECK-Vidya • Healing the Past through Dreams • Reasons for Loneliness • Claims by Others • Past-Life Readings

5. **Family Relationships** 69

Finding True Love • Responsibilities to Your Family • When to Share with a Mate • Staying Free through Charity • Two Paths, One Marriage • When Your Family Is Hurting • How Does ECKANKAR View Sex? • Why Virginity until Marriage? • When Your Children Are Hurting • Your Children's Experiences • When a Loved One Dies • The Truth about Twins • Anger in Families • Helping Others in Your Family • Can You Love Your Family Too Much?

6. **Balance and Harmony** 87

Why Is Your Life Hard? • An ECK Secret • Inner Harmony • Overcome Procrastination • How to Avoid Unconscious Karma • Soul's Path to Mastership • When You See Your Future • Balancing the Blues • Having Patience • Financial Balance • Can You Serve ECK Too Much? • Balance in Helping Others • Lessons That Teach Balance • Do You Belong on This Path? • The Way to See Truth • Making Peace with Yourself • How Do You Stay in Balance?

7. **Questions about ECK** 103

What's the Purpose of ECK? • Can ECK Help You? • Will Your Life Change? • How Will You Feel? • Will ECK Make a Difference in Your Life? • Hungry for Truth • What Is a Co-worker with God? • The Call of Soul • A Question of Balance • Experiences in the Light and Sound • Can You Follow Two Paths? • Make Your Own Decisions • Proof You Are Soul • For Those Who Want God • Which Path Is the Right One?

8. **Change and Growth** 117

Spiritual Progress • Cave of Purification • Are You Still Growing? • What about Physical Limitations? • Surrender • Evolution of Ideas • Do You Feel Unworthy?

• Fear of Change • An Instrument of Change • Cycles of Change • What Mistakes Mean • Finding Your Personal Pace

9. Creativity and Self-Discipline 127
Self-Discipline and Inertia • Resisting Downward Pulls • Does Smoking Affect Your Spiritual Growth? • Fasting from Bad Habits • Facing Yourself Honestly • Your Spiritual Survival • When to Take Action, When Not • Answering Spiritual Questions • Initiate Reports • Action as Self-Discipline • Privilege of Life • The Purpose of Music • Write Down Your Experiences • Creative Success • Why ECK Writers? • Creative Channels

10. Spiritual Goals 147
Spiritual Purpose • Are You a Co-worker with God? • Spiritual Goal Setting • After the Fifth Initiation • Thinking from the End • How Can You Be a Lover of Life? • Finding Your Cycle • Spiritual Success • Conscious Evolution • Spiritual Goals and Religions • When Others Leave ECK

11. Soul Travel 163
Desire to Soul Travel • Putting Your Experiences into Words • Simplify Your Experience • How Do You Use Your Imagination? • Uses of Soul Travel • Do Animals Soul Travel? • When You Don't Remember • Human Reactions • Beyond Soul Travel • Soul and the Bodies • Can Soul Get Lost? • Can You Overcome Fear of Soul Travel? • Protection during Soul Travel • Belief in Your Experiences • When You Pass On

12. The ECK Masters 181
Inner and Outer Master • Why Do the ECK Masters Serve? • Only One Mahanta • Blue Star • Presence of the Master • Three Aspects of God • Friends • A Continuous Line of Masters • The Spiritual Hierarchy • How Is the Mahanta Chosen? • Who Are the ECK Masters? • Master Compilers • Journey to Mastership • Tests of the Masters

Glossary 201

Introduction

Each week Sri Harold Klemp receives letters from all over the world. ECKists, and students from many different spiritual paths, ask his advice on how to navigate the perils and adventures of the spiritual life. His letters in reply show them how to make everyday living more joyful.

Ask the Master, Book 1, is the first compilation of questions and answers from Sri Harold's personal correspondence. A very few have been previously published in columns in the *Mystic World* or *Letter of Light,* but over 90 percent are from his private letters.

The book's twelve chapters answer questions about dreams, spiritual protection, problem solving, and relationships with others. In them are useful clues: how to achieve balance and harmony, recognize a past life, chart personal change and growth, and develop creativity and self-discipline.

Although most of the correspondence is personal, between Master and chela, the message is universal. The desire of the seeker to know God, despite all obstacles, is seen in the heartfelt questions the Master receives. His compassion for every Soul on the way home to God is revealed in the insightful answers.

Dreams are like a daily report card. They show you how you are doing in your spiritual mission, even if you don't know you have one. Dreams tell how you are getting on with Divine Spirit and life.

1

Dreams

My dream state is very active, and I wake up remembering at least one dream. What does this mean spiritually?

Most people are in a daze but don't know it. They have hardly any idea about their life in the higher spiritual worlds while their body lies asleep at day's end.

Dreams are like a daily report card. They show how you are doing in your spiritual mission, even if you don't know you have one. Dreams tell how you are getting on with Divine Spirit and life.

Are Dreams Real?

I understand that while dreaming, we are actually Soul traveling. Therefore, the places I go in my dreams are real and so are the instances that occur. If the people in my dreams are also real, does that mean there are other people having the same dream as me?

A dream is a real experience. Soul Travel is a more-than-real spiritual experience.

As Soul, you can (and do) have hundreds of experiences going on side by side at different levels. So does everyone else.

Here is a way to understand the variety of inner experiences: it's as if Soul experiences what hundreds of people in a town do on a certain day. The mind, meanwhile, can recall only a few experiences at a time.

You may remember a certain inner experience with someone on the inner planes because of its spiritual importance for you. However, the other person will likely remember a completely different experience, because your needs are different.

In comparison to Soul, our mind holds only a few memories at a time. We remember those that mean the most to us spiritually.

Only rarely do the spiritual needs of two people exactly coincide. When they do, both dreamers will remember the same dream. However, their different levels of consciousness will give each a special view of what actually happened in the dream state.

What does the dream state represent that the waking state does not?

There is no difference in my mind. Each person is Soul, capable of being fully aware twenty-four hours a day. The lessons of life come to us every minute, on every level. However, few people today pay much mind to the power of Soul and Its being. The average person goes through life with only the barest sense of his or her true identity as Soul, a spark of God.

Start Remembering Your Dreams

I wish I could remember my dreams better. Can you help?

2

Some people naturally enjoy vivid recollections of their dream state, but those who don't can develop the skill. There are several things one must do to remember dreams.

First, there must be a great desire that is love and goodwill at the heart center during the spiritual exercises. Keep a happy thought of some past event or the like. Keep a notebook and pen by your bedside, and make a resolution to wake—even in the middle of the night—to record any memory of the dream state, no matter how trivial it seems.

The following statement is a way to seek help from the Inner Master at bedtime: "I give you permission to take me to that Temple of Golden Wisdom I have earned or wherever you wish." This is usually successful after some time.

What are your dreams like?

I no longer refer to my Soul journeys as dreams. In the past, yes, I did dream.

Now my journeys into the spiritual worlds are crystal clear, without the sense of distortion so common to dreams. That's why I prefer to call my dreams Soul journeys. But I do study an inner event and try to see what message it might hold for my waking life.

How do you interpret them?

There are key dreams (I'll call them dreams) that tell me about problems at work. One group of such dreams has to do with baseball.

If the playing field is in top condition as at a major-league stadium, then all is well. Usually it's not. Then the location of the field might be partly in a woods and partly in a cow pasture. The bases are at odd distances

from each other, and often out of sight. It means something in my daily life is not in balance, and I'd better
find out where and how the situation got so out of
shape.

Open Your Spiritual Eye

*Once when I was awakening from the dream state,
it felt as though I was receiving a mild electric shock.
Was my body being attacked by some entity, or is this
a natural state of reentering the body?*

This was done to key your awareness to what was
happening. Although you remember this incident clearly
now, you would not have done so without the extra
energy.

The electrical shock was more than a prod to remember the dream. The Mahanta will give the initiate
spiritual shocks when it is necessary to open the
Spiritual Eye. Much of the time this passes unnoticed;
but nevertheless, it is true all the same. Your body was
not being attacked by an entity.

This is why the ECK Masters tell people that only
the bold and adventurous will see God. There are a lot
of things in the inner worlds that would have frightened even saints from the Middle Ages. There is nothing to fear, as most inner experiences of this nature
come once and then are gone.

Increased Dream Awareness

*Why can't the chela be aware of all his dreams? I
do not recall meeting the Mahanta in the dream state.
Why do I forget the inner teachings when I awaken in
the morning?*

The physical mind is limited, like a little bucket. The inner experiences you have on all the planes are like the vast ocean. It is useless trying to pour the ocean into the mind's little bucket.

Soul is running several bodies at the same time on other planes. Its scope of action is much greater than the recall ability of the dreamer's mind.

Recognition of the Inner Master takes some people longer than others. The spiritual exercises are aided by the Friday fasts in opening the Spiritual Eye. The fasts are to be done under a doctor's care if there is any physical problem. Briefly, the three fasts are: the mental fast—keeping attention completely upon the Inner Master; the partial fast—only one meal, or else fruit juices and fruit; and the water fast for a twenty-four-hour period.

These fasts are one way to remember the dream state.

What is a spiritual dream?

A spiritual dream is any dream. There is a spiritual side to every experience or event, no matter how large or small, and whether or not it occurs in everyday life or in a dream.

But,—and this is a big *but*—few people have the spiritual eyes to see.

When You Dream about the ECK Masters

One night I had a beautiful dream. I went with Wah Z, the Dream Master, to a place where there was a huge castle and a blue sun. The ECK Master Rebazar Tarzs came flying out of the sun and landed in front of us. Then he, Wah Z, and I went into the castle. Inside I saw every ECK Master and heard a beautiful flute

5

playing. I wondered where it was coming from. Then I saw a blue light and followed it until I came to a door where bright light shone around the edges. I opened the door and saw the ECK Master Yaubl Sacabi playing the flute. Where was this?

I'm glad you remembered your visit to the place of the huge castle and blue sun. It is on the Mental Plane. Rebazar Tarzs coming out of the sun meant out of the heart of SUGMAD. The castle is actually one of the Golden Wisdom Temples. This is the reason why you saw all the ECK Masters there. They come to teach Souls to hear and see the Sound and Light of God.

Some people think that Paul Twitchell, the founder of ECKANKAR, and I made up the idea about real ECK Masters, like Rebazar Tarzs, Yaubl Sacabi, and the rest. They still have to learn how to love the ECK, Divine Spirit, above all things, the way you do. Otherwise the ECK Masters cannot take them into the beautiful worlds of ECK. Keep on doing the spiritual exercises, and I will be with you.

I do not remember seeing any of the past ECK Masters physically or in the dream state. We have a picture of you, but I haven't seen you in my dreams, either. Sometimes in my dreams, I have traveled with someone, but I never really see his face. Why is this?

The "someone" you travel with in your dreams is an ECK Master, whose name you will learn in time. It is not important now.

Why don't you see the ECK Masters? It is your inner self throwing a ring of protection around your lower-world fears. Fear makes us put off the Spiritual Exercises of ECK. Why? Because we are secretly afraid something out of the ordinary might happen. Maybe

6

the Mahanta would really come in person. What would we say to him? That's fear of unworthiness.

But when the Master does come, the experience is simply different than anything the mind could mock up. The Master is found to be quite a good friend, and you feel naturally comfortable with him. This is what the person in the grip of fear doesn't know, so the meetings with the Inner Master are delayed until the student is more reasonable in his thinking about what sort of being the Master really is.

Here I'll say that you are already meeting nightly with him. It is only a matter of time until you remember. My love is always with you.

Invite the Mahanta Along

I had a dream in which I was walking down a sidewalk with a friend at 9:00 p.m. I looked up in the sky and saw the moon, which looked huge. Beside the moon was a big planet with a ring around it. Everyone else in the dream seemed to take no notice but carried on as if it were just an ordinary day. I was excited and wanted to know why the moon and planet were there. Can you please explain to me what this dream means?

Yours is a spiritual dream.

The sidewalk is the path of ECK. Since it's your dream and your path, the lessons will be yours—not your friend's. Evening means the end of Soul's karmic day: this life is your gateway to spiritual freedom. Looking up into the sky indicates your high spiritual vision. The huge moon is the promise of a brighter life in ECK, here and now.

The big planet with the ring is a symbol for the great worlds of ECK beyond our own. You alone, of all the others in the dream, were thrilled at the sight of the moon and planet because of your appreciation for spiritual things. Overall, the dream means you may go with the Mahanta to the spiritual worlds of ECK.

If you would like to see them, say at bedtime, "Wah Z, show me the wonder of SUGMAD's creation."

Dreams within Dreams

Sometimes when I am dreaming, I wake up to find I am still dreaming. And I wake up again to find myself waking up in yet another dream. I have counted as many as fifteen or twenty of these awakenings before I am awake on the outer. What is this experience?

This is an excellent sign of your spiritual growth.

Soul can run a number of bodies at one time. For instance, the Astral Plane has about 150 distinct levels, or heavens, in it; Soul may materialize a body in any number of those subplanes. The Causal Plane is described as having many more levels than that. Therefore, in the Soul body, you may actually run twenty or more bodies at once in the other worlds.

During the process of waking up, Soul is returning from these far places, and you may momentarily remember each of your inner bodies in turn. By the time you wake up here, your attention is completely nested in your physical body again for everyday life at school, work, or home.

The multiple awakenings show your developing growth in the worlds of God. You've made a good start in ECK.

Lucid Dreaming

What is the difference between lucid dreaming and Soul Travel?

Lucid dreaming is the experience of an individual on the Astral Plane, which lies right above the Physical Plane.

Soul Travel goes beyond lucid dreaming. It is a journey one can make not only to the Astral Plane, but to any of the planes above it: the Causal, Mental, Etheric, and Soul planes. But to have a true Soul Travel experience, a dreamer needs the help of the Mahanta, the Dream Master. The Mahanta is head of the ECK Adepts, a band of spiritual travelers, and has the spiritual power to take a dreamer far beyond the Astral Plane.

Jumping through Experiences

I was having a dream about one thing, and some other dream jumped in and interrupted. In fact, about five different dreams did that. I was dreaming about being in a pasture and then some ninjas jumped out and attacked me. What does this mean, if anything? Why do dreams do that?

Dreams do not really jump in on each other at all. What happens is that in the Soul body you are jumping from one inner experience to another.

Soul can be in several different places at the same time. This is not unusual, because Soul runs at least one body on each of the lower planes, and sometimes more. What you see as skipping from one dream to another is like switching TV channels to see what programs are on. Such skipping about gets old, so we usually settle down to watch whatever interests us the most, like your dream of the ninjas.

Your experience with the ninjas in that dream world was real. When we watch violence on TV, it means we are in agreement with it inwardly. This opens us to nightmares. It's better to watch happier programs or read uplifting books, if we want more restful dreams.

Is It Real, or Is It a Symbol?

How can I tell whether the people I meet in the dream state are other Souls or just symbolic parts of myself?

The dream world and its people are real. It is only our recall and understanding of it that are incomplete. Our link with the inner worlds is usually through dreams, but illusion can make our memory of inner events faulty.

What about the dream people who appear to be just symbolic parts of ourselves? Let's start with the waking dream. The Mahanta uses it to give someone a spiritual insight from an experience in his daily life. The Master draws on the individual's experiences with real people and real events to point out some personal truth.

Apply the principle of the waking dream to your dream world. The people you meet there are Souls, just like you. However, the Mahanta can turn your experiences with them into an open window of understanding, to unlock your desires, needs, and goals.

Admittedly, ECKANKAR is nearly alone in treating the dream world as real. More paths and teachings will someday reach the same understanding, but only after their people travel consciously in the other worlds as many ECKists do.

Protect Yourself from Nightmares

I am twelve years old. I had a bad dream where I was attacked by Kal, the negative power, in the form of bad vibrations from a cartoon on TV. I would like to know how to avoid frightening dreams like that in the future. Thank you.

To avoid frightening dreams caused by a certain cartoon on TV, watch other cartoons instead. Don't let anything into your life that hurts or frightens you, if you can do something about it. That means not just a cartoon show, but also people, food, habits, etc. You'll be much more at peace with yourself.

Dream Tests

In a dream I saw myself in a class that looked like an auditorium. After class, one of my friends and I went up to the teacher, who said he could only give truth to people thirty-three years of age or more. Since I was fifty, I told him I qualified. Others in the dream later gave me encouragement. Is the Mahanta involved in this dream?

In a second dream, a so-called holy man brought gifts to my two friends and me. They took them, but I did not. I refused because the Mahanta did not give me the gifts. What does this dream mean?

In the first dream, the teacher was a spokesman for the Mahanta. The teacher set an artificial qualification of acceptance: he would accept no one younger than thirty-three years of age. It was an easy qualifier, which fit your age. But you yourself had to state, "I am qualified to learn truth." It is Soul's commitment to the ways of Divine Spirit.

The second dream was to test your sincerity. Were you really ready to follow the Mahanta or was this just another spiritual shopping trip? You refused the lesser

11

gifts, even though your friends accepted them, because you desired only the Master's gifts.

Your Dream Sword

In a dream, I had left my body and was flying. I was holding a sword that gave me a lot of energy and made me feel like a child. It was guiding me. When I let go of it, it was as though I lost the energy and began falling back toward my body. Eventually I didn't have to hold the sword anymore but just had it by my side.

The sword is your secret word.

The Mahanta puts energy into your secret word and makes it what it is. Once he establishes this power in your word, one more thing is needed to make it work: your attention. Thereafter this word can lift you into the secret world of dreams. Your secret word connects you with the ECK, which then guides you everywhere. However, should your attention lapse, the dream comes to a swift end and you reenter the body.

With practice, your word becomes so much a part of you that you sing it in time of need without a second thought.

Fear of Death in Dreams

I have had a recurring dream ever since I was a child. I'm taking a bath, and a hand falls into the tub and grabs my toe. I usually wake up screaming, very scared and having trouble breathing. What does this dream mean?

Your dream about a hand falling in the bathtub and grabbing your toe is, oddly enough, a spiritual dream. It shows a deep fear of dying, even though outwardly

12

few people would guess that of you.

Taking a bath sets the dream up as meaning: Be ready; this is a spiritual dream. For water often means something spiritual. Being in the bathtub means you're immersed in thoughts of a spiritual nature. But then the hand falls into the tub. It's not a normal hand, but a *disembodied* one. *Disembodied* here means death. The hand grabs your toe, the very end of your body. That means, "In the end death will get you."

Once you understand that this is a spiritual dream, you will find its power over you will lessen. The Spiritual Exercises of ECK will prove to you that Soul never dies.

Controlling Your Life

I dreamed I was in a car and I was eating, paying no attention to the fact that the car was driving very safely on its own. When I noticed that the car was moving, I thought, Boy, am I lucky to have the Mahanta taking care of me. I then decided to take control of the car and drive it myself. When I did this, the seat moved back so I couldn't reach the steering wheel and the windshield got all foggy. I barely kept from hitting a truck.

Yours is a very good spiritual dream. The car, of course, is your life. The eating means doing the spiritual exercises and living the life of ECK.

Anyone who does the Spiritual Exercises of ECK finds his life runs very well because the unseen driver is the Mahanta. You know this. Trouble begins when one sees how well things are going and then takes credit for it. That's the ego getting behind the wheel. The seat moved back means that the ego and mind are too far away from spiritual control (the steering wheel)

13

to be able to run things right. The foggy windshield means the clouded vision of the ego, or the human self.

ECK dreams give a personal look at where you are now in ECK. The Mahanta uses them to tell the chela how well he is unfolding. Write down your dreams and study them. They will give you all the direction in life you need.

What can dreams tell us about ourselves?

Dreams hint at truth. I say *hint* instead of *tell* for a reason: Most people don't actually want to know the truth. The truth hurts. Dreams can tell us when we're unkind, unfair, vengeful, selfish, and other unpleasant facts that we need to work on spiritually. But truth makes most people uncomfortable, so they shut it out and forget their dreams.

I've tried many dream systems and have kept a record of my own inner travels for years. Of all the systems, the dream methods of ECK are the golden thread that have been of the most use to me for spiritual growth.

Falling Sensations

I used to have an experience that I wish you would explain. Whenever I was waking up from sleep, I would feel as though I were falling from a great height and as if I were out of my body. I was never afraid because I felt familiar with the vibrations of those heights. What was most interesting was the beautiful music I always heard. Often I heard madrigals, with mostly female voices.

When you were waking up, Soul was coming back to the body from the higher planes. This gave you the feeling of falling from a great height and was a Soul Travel experience.

Hearing the madrigal indicates Soul Travel on the Mental Plane, since this form of song particularly develops the Mental body. The madrigal is another expression of the Sound Current there in addition to the sound of running water. This experience shows you are being prepared for the high spiritual planes in this lifetime.

Dreams Are Subtle

I would like to know what to do to remember more details from my dreams. Are there any practices that would help this?

One's unfoldment goes through different stages at the direction of the Mahanta. Soul gets what is best for It, and this depends on how faithfully one practices the Spiritual Exercises of ECK.

It is possible to develop a sharper recall of the dream state by keeping a notebook by the bed, with pen and light at hand. As one unfolds, the inner experiences get more subtle. Perhaps all that's needed is to increase our recall to keep pace with the subtleties.

Sharing Dreams

My wife and son had a dream the same night about the same subject. Both were bitten on the foot: my wife, by snakes; my son, by a monster. Is it possible to share the same dream? And what does it mean in the dream state to step on things like animals or to lose one's shoes? I've had dreams about misplacing my shoes and cannot start an important activity until I find them.

Two people can indeed share the same dream, especially when there is a close affinity between them. To your wife, the snake bites mean to watch for hidden or missing clauses in contracts that pertain to the building and furnishing of your new home. Watch for "snakes in the grass." The monster biting your son means for him to be aware of more obvious accidents around the home, such as the one he suffered recently. If attention is put upon the Mahanta, these minor irritations can be avoided, for they need never be more than that.

To step on things like animals means to be careful not to hurt the feelings of others by thoughtlessness. The image of animals, which are often thought to be inferior to man, means a lack of sensitivity to those on the perimeter of our own consciousness.

Misplaced shoes or articles of clothing that prevent one from keeping important appointments mean that one's inner life has outpaced his outer life. He must immediately set new goals in his daily life. This is so both worlds are brought into balance again; otherwise, he will be left with a gnawing feeling of misplacement. I hope this gives you an idea of how one approaches the interpretation of dreams.

Soul's Freedom

I walked up into some hills, and it seemed like the Fourth of July. Thousands of people were sitting in the hills looking into the sky as if expecting fireworks. The sky was light blue and free of clouds.

I walked past the crowds until I was alone again and looked at the hills in the distance. They were like hard-packed sand dunes without vegetation. Suddenly, a flash of red went by and stopped long enough for me

16

to recognize it before disappearing. It was me. That made me feel really odd. Looking out over the ridge of hills, I saw that they had undergone a drastic change. They were much lumpier, and a huge boulder with green vines all over it had been raised ten feet into the air.

The dream felt very real. I had just gone through a doorway and was expecting a member of an ancient American race that I had just read about in a Louis L'Amour novel. But I woke up before he arrived.

This is what your dream means: Your walk up into the hills indicates that in the dream you were moving into a higher state of consciousness.

The Fourth of July is Independence Day. The Dream Master used this image to evoke in you the ideal of spiritual freedom, which you can achieve in this lifetime if you set your heart upon it.

The thousands of people are your collective awareness—i.e., the sum total of your thoughts and hopes. You are awaiting the ecstasy of spiritual freedom. The blue sky signifies the Blue Light of the Mahanta. When you leave the crowds, it means you leave behind your worries and come to rest in Soul, the center of your being.

You are now in the Soul body and look back on the hills, which are nothing more than events in your daily life. From the lofty vantage point of Soul, your outer life seems to be a spiritual wasteland, especially when you let anger (the "flash of red") flare up.

The image of the boulder is used in a double sense here. First, Soul studies the ridge of hills to see what harm anger might do, and It perceives a "much lumpier" life. Anger makes mountains out of molehills, or in this case, a huge boulder is raised ten feet into the air.

Second, green vines clinging to the face of the

17

boulder show the power of envy or jealousy to undermine a relationship. Have you heard the phrase "green with envy"? The roots of the vines can, in time, shatter the greatest boulder, just as envy and jealousy can destroy the closest relationship, even one that seems "solid as a rock."

The member of an ancient American race whom you were expecting was the Mahanta, the Living ECK Master.

This dream gives a most exacting look at yourself. It shows how the Master may shape your dream to help you better understand yourself.

How can one explore other parts of oneself in the dream state?

The ECK Masters say that a person is spiritually of six parts: the Physical, the Astral (emotions), the Causal (memory of past lives), the Mental (thought), the Etheric (intuition), and Soul (the eternal).

In the ECK teachings, there is a sacred word for each level. For example, if you want to look at a past life, the word to sing for a few minutes at bedtime is Mana (say MAH-nah). Other special words are in *The Spiritual Notebook* by Paul Twitchell.

It often takes a month to see a past-life experience, so don't give up the first day. You must have a very strong desire to see your past.

Familiar Dream Worlds

I would like to know the meaning of déjà vu. *Recently, I have quite often been struck by pictures or remembrances of things I have already seen or lived. Could it be that I dreamed my entire life before?*

18

Déjà vu is a strong feeling of already having experienced something before.

Life is a dream from beginning to end. Some people, like you, have the unusual ability of bringing the memory of a dream into the present moment. That is the reason so many things are already familiar to you. It is a special ability, but remember that other people have their special gifts too. That's why this world is such an interesting place to live.

Preparing for Your Future

I had a dream in which I found myself in a meeting at the ECK Center of the city to which I will be moving. There was only one ECKist there that I knew, and he was acting very out of character. The atmosphere was disturbing. Nothing was getting accomplished because ECK chelas were interrupting each other and not paying attention. The meeting decayed, and I left.

Then I went through the city to the waterfront, where I walked along the water on a narrow boardwalk. Suddenly a storm blew in, and the water began getting rough, rocking the boardwalk. I realized I would probably be thrown into the water, and sure enough, the whole walk was soon overturned by the waves. The boards flipped over me and pinned me under the surface.

I relaxed, telling myself I could probably work myself free. But I tried and couldn't. Then I panicked, heaving up to try to reach air. As I strained frantically, I awoke in bed in a cold sweat.

No person, place, or thing is perfect. Keep this in mind when you move to the new city. The way of doing things at the ECK Center there will certainly be different from what you are used to now.

19

How easy it is to mistake "different" for "wrong." We get caught up in our own ideas of right and wrong. If we become self-righteous on top of that, we find we are less tolerant in a new place, and everything seems to line up against us. Certainly, the last place most of us think to look for the cause of our grievances is inside ourselves, but that is usually the exact source of our problems.

Go to your new city with an open mind. What sense is there in trying to change everyone else in the new ECK Center when it's so much easier to change ourselves? Intolerance hurts us every time.

There is nothing in this dream you can't handle.

Dreams about Ancient Times

I haven't been having any dreams that I can remember for the past month. This is unusual for me; I usually have dreams all the time. Is it karma? I would like to know, if possible, because I learn from my dreams.

Another thing I would like to know is are there knights on the higher planes? I am attracted to medieval wars and battles.

In answer to your first question: By the time you read this, you will have started to dream again. There are times when Soul shifts gears; this is when we don't always remember our dreams. But it is a passing thing.

About your attraction to knights and medieval wars and battles: Your interest in that period of history is due to your many past lives there. It was a time of great adventure, chivalry, and heroics. The forces of darkness and light were in a hotly contested battle for

20

centuries, and you played a part in those unsettled, but interesting, times.

History can teach us much about how mankind's unlearned lessons repeat themselves. This allows us to use our knowledge to avoid unnecessary problems, because we can sidestep a lot of them.

People make history. You might enjoy the historical novels of Mary Stewart that bring to life the times of King Arthur at the beginning of the Middle Ages: *The Crystal Cave, The Hollow Hills, The Last Enchantment,* and *The Wicked Day.* You'll find many spiritual insights in her books, for she is adept at looking at past-life records on the Causal Plane. The books are in the library.

I recently had a dream in which a man taught me some important things about life. He exuded as much love as an ECK Master. At first, I thought he was an ECK Master in disguise. But his name was Merlin the Priest, and he lived in an old room which contained many Arthurian relics.

Was Merlin an ECK Master? Thank you.

Merlin was an actual person. In her novels, Mary Stewart draws a fairly good picture of his life during sixth-century England. You can find *The Crystal Cave* and *The Hollow Hills* in many libraries.

He was not an ECK Master while the adviser of King Arthur, nor is he now. Yet, Merlin has continued his search for truth in the other worlds and does know some members of the Vairagi Order. He is ready to share his knowledge of the ancient mysteries with all who prove themselves worthy.

First, however, they need to find his home in a remote forest on the Astral Plane.

Are You Ready to Begin?

*I have had two dreams with a man who asked me,
"Are you ready to begin your journey yet?" Who is he?*

You are willing to love without conditions, and this
frame of mind is needed for Soul Travel. The Master
you met sometimes is near Yaubl Sacabi; they look like
brothers.

His name can be gotten by asking him who he is
the next time he comes.

Learning New Laws

*I have always trusted my dreams and made most
of my decisions based on them. Since becoming a Fifth
Initiate, I have had several dreams that did not manifest the way I dreamed them. This is a great crisis for
me, since I now feel I cannot be a channel for the ECK.
Please help me find the truth.*

About your concern that you can no longer interpret your dreams as before the Fifth Initiation: Remember your experience with me on the inner planes?
That is the Mahanta telling you that your spiritual life
is in good shape.

So why can you not trust your dreams any longer?
You're being taken to a higher level of understanding
life: by seeing, knowing, and being. Because the
Mahanta no longer lets you lean on dreams to make
judgments about others, you are faced with the necessity of giving someone a chance to help the ECK works
without being able to refuse their help because of a
dream. That means you are now put in a position of
looking at a person objectively.

From now on it means that trust comes first on
your part. On the other hand, the other person is given

a chance to earn that trust. You decide on the worth of a person because of what he actually does, not what you think he might do wrong.

Go ahead and learn all you can about the spiritual laws of the Fifth Plane. They are certainly different from those on the Fourth. But you'll get the hang of it before you know it.

Serving Others in Dreams

I have had several dreams where I am talking to groups of people about ECKANKAR. In one dream I held a roving microphone for others to ask you questions. In the past people have told me that I have helped them in their dreams. I would appreciate some insight into this. Am I, as Soul, really doing these things?

It was good to hear that you are remembering some of the service you are able to give on the inner planes. The Higher Initiate helps with the works of ECK on the spiritual planes, teaching Satsang classes and assisting at ECK seminars. To many, this would be beyond comprehension.

When the individual first steps on the path of ECK, he generally confronts past-life experiences that emerge in the dream state through symbols. The censor is quite protective of the emotional states and will garble the past-life experience in order not to upset the initiate. The Inner Master thus pulls the curtain on the past lives or other lessons.

So many who ask for remembrance of these experiences are actually receiving protection while certain karma works itself out by having scenes blotted from memory.

As one unfolds higher into the God Worlds through further initiations, the inner experiences become less phenomenal. Soul is gradually being led from the phenomenal worlds toward the worlds of true being at the Soul Plane and beyond.

Yet, some feel unhappy when they no longer have the experiences that date back to their spiritual childhood. It is like a high-school student demanding to become a first grader again because he was happier then. Life always takes us forward if we will go.

Regarding the point of others seeing the Higher Initiate helping them on the inner planes: Frequently the Mahanta is not able to work with the individual directly. Thus the ECK takes the matrix of the Higher Initiate, with whom the individual has established a rapport. That is the only way possible to bring upliftment in consciousness. Since it is the ECK working and not the personality of the Higher Initiate, the Higher Initiate is frequently not aware of the meeting.

I appreciate your help in presenting the message of ECK.

The Gentle Way of Dreaming

I recently decided to become an ECKist. But I am having difficulty with Soul Travel and my dreams because I cannot stop worrying over details of my physical life. Please, I need your help.

I greatly appreciate your letter about lack of spiritual success. A good attitude is that ECKANKAR influences the individual's life. Put forth every effort to learn and grow during the lessons of the day with a light attention on the presence of the Inner Master.

The point is: Carry out the physical duties and responsibilities as if you're doing them for God.

Do the Spiritual Exercises of ECK as you usually

do them, but at bedtime give a thought request to the Inner Master, with love and goodwill in the heart center: "I give you permission to take me to wherever you see I've earned the right." Then go peacefully to sleep without giving all this another thought.

You can vary the phrasing every few weeks for the benefit of the mind, which likes the stimulation of new ideas.

Sometimes we try too hard and push against the doors of Soul, forgetting that the doors open inwardly and cannot be forced. The spiritual exercises work best if one can fill himself with love and goodwill by thinking of someone who makes him happy.

This gentle technique can bring one to a conscious awakening in the dream state.

Three Steps for Better Dreaming

What instruction, advice, or technique would you give someone on how to sleep properly, so he can make use of the period when his body is stilled and leave it to travel in the upper regions with his teacher?

There are three main steps I recommend. First, arrange your schedule to get as much sleep as needed to be fresh in the morning.

Second, for a few minutes before sleeping, read from any of the ECK books to signal Soul of your intent to pursue spiritual activity during sleep: for example *The Eternal Dreamer, The Dream Master, The Shariyat-Ki-Sugmad, The Spiritual Notebook,* or *Stranger by the River.*

Third, contemplate upon the face of the Mahanta, the Living ECK Master at bedtime. Do this in either a seated or prone position. In the spiritual exercise, give an invitation to the Master like this: "I welcome you into my heart as into my home. Please enter it with joy."

Then go to sleep as usual, but leave the eye of Soul alert to the coming of the teacher. Look for me, because I am always with you.

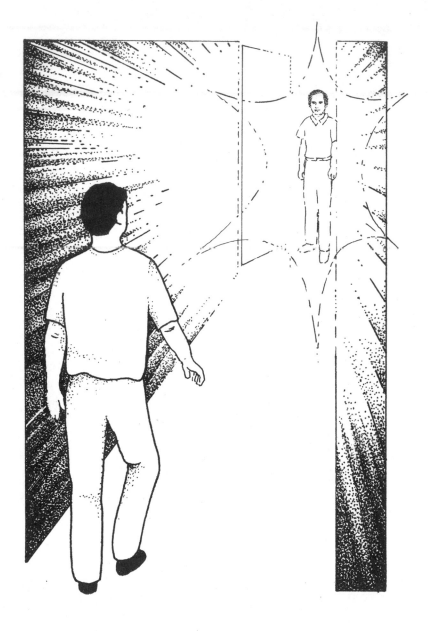

Divine Spirit opens up new opportunities, but we must take them. The ECK Masters lead the inexperienced Soul to self-mastery by awakening love in one's heart.

2

Spiritual Protection

I've read about ECK miracles and have been asking for your help. Why don't I see results?

While it is true that some people get help from the ECK in a flashy, outward way, many people do not. What have we earned? Just asking for God's gift does not bring it. Jesus said, while offering help to the sick, "According to your faith be it unto you." According to your faith . . .

Divine Spirit opens up new opportunities, but we must take them. The ECK Masters lead the inexperienced Soul to self-mastery by awakening love in one's heart. You must make your own choices with the best information at hand. Only then can Spirit help and guide you in your decisions.

How Are ECKists Protected?

My husband and I feel we are under psychic attack much of the time. We took a course in another line of teaching and learned that many of our problems are caused by those outside ourselves. I thought that being ECKists protected us from this sort of thing.

I appreciated your letter about the subject of psychic attacks. One must keep in mind that earth is a training ground for Soul to open Itself as a vehicle for Divine Spirit. What then blocks Soul from instantly recognizing Itself in Self- and God-Realization? Not yet knowing how to control the five passions of the mind.

We personally are responsible for our own state of consciousness. That results in a particular series of situations in our life. As Soul unfolds toward total freedom, It understands total responsibility must be accepted for every thought and action.

Mixing two different paths splits our consciousness. We owe it to our own spiritual development to choose a path to God, whatever it is, and live it.

If psychic attacks bother us, it's because sometime in the past we have opened the door. If it's a real problem, one must seek licensed counseling. *The Shariyat-Ki-Sugmad,* Book Two, pages 56–60 and page 137, gives insight in reasons surrounding psychic attacks.

Domes of Energy

I've heard about the domes of protection that surround an ECKist's home. Is this protection there even if not everyone in the household is an ECKist?

The domes of protective energy around ECKists' homes are there regardless, even if one of the members of the household does not live the ECK life.

30

Personal Protection

I live with another person who uses drugs. My question is perhaps a tedious one for ECKists who know that ECK and drugs do not mix. How can drug abuse affect others living under the same roof, who are ECKists, who do not share the habit, and who are not aware when this is happening?

The love and protection of the ECK are with you in all spiritual concerns. In regard to the effect that a user of recreational drugs has upon others who live with him but do not use drugs themselves, the full responsibility for any karma created by such an act is borne by the user of drugs alone. He is also held accountable if others should stumble on the path to God because of his self-indulgent appetite for drugs.

Only his own aura is pierced, but when his karmic load is increased by the Lords of Karma, naturally it will also have a secondhand effect upon all who are near to him, although he must bear his own punishments.

The answer I'm giving you here is only part of the full answer to your situation. The other part will be given by the Inner Master and may be consciously recalled upon awakening in the morning or not. Nevertheless, be assured that the Mahanta is now starting to resolve the situation for your spiritual benefit. Watch closely how Divine Spirit does this, for Its ways are beyond the ways of men.

Protection from Others

I have been aware that members of a religious group I used to be involved in are still trying to get me under their influence. Besides outer ways—mail and

31

phone calls—they are appearing in my dreams. I would like to know how to protect myself from them.

There are several means of protection that are possible to use against those who intrude into our state of being. One simple method is putting a reversed mirror between yourself and the harm. This is done by imagining a mockup of a mirror that reflects back to the sender all unwanted thoughts and forces.

Another form of self-protection is to put yourself in a white circle of light. Then look out from this center at whatever is disturbing you. You may also imagine a wall that shields you from the psychic enemy.

Those are inward solutions. If you find the need, do whatever is necessary on the physical level. In case they are able to bother you physically, it may be necessary to ask for protection from the legal authorities. When the force is all subtle, consider calling competent counseling and tell them what is troubling you. Ask what, if anything, can be done for you. The local hospital ought to be able to give you the names of licensed counselors.

The Holy Spirit often works through professional medical people to help us out when we're in trouble. After all, all healing comes from Divine Spirit, no matter what It chooses as Its instrument.

Freedom from Suffering

I've let my fears really mess me up. Should my goal always be to choose my own way of life no matter what others think of my decisions? Deep down, I know this is true, and yet it's hard to break loose of that feeling that insists I must suffer in this life.

Thank you for your letter. In general, let me say

that people will intrude upon our good nature for their own negative purposes if we let them.

It is simply a matter of catching them at their game, then slowly but gradually, over a period of time, letting ourselves be less accessible to them.

It is part of the freedom we can develop for ourselves by adopting a different attitude about What will people think? With practice, we get better at handling the subtle pressures and guilts that are thrown at us, especially if someone is attempting to bend our will to fit their own.

Often, it is enough to chant HU inwardly and silently whenever in the presence of a person who is intruding into our psychic space. Singing HU either opens us to direct help from Divine Spirit or else gives us the insight on how to handle the next step in this situation ourselves.

I want you to know that the love and protection of the ECK is always with you.

Shifting Your Attention

A member of my family has always tried to get me involved with black magic. Lately she has involved herself in a group of psychics who are projecting fear and control toward me, my son, and my daughter. I never made the connection until my daughter spoke of the voices she kept hearing. In addition to asking for your help, I am practicing the presence of the Mahanta and putting a constant Blue Light around us.

The only harm that can come to us is that which we allow to happen. To strengthen the spiritual foundation, may I suggest that you and your children either do a HU Song or a spiritual exercise together every morning and evening. Also be aware of what kind of rest the children are getting; make sure it is enough right now.

Get into some outside activities that are fun for all of you, if possible. The libraries often have leads on what to do. Whatever you do, put your full attention on the Inner Master, but also get your attention on the brighter things in life. If you fill your consciousness with the positive aspects of Divine Spirit, there is no vacuum where the negative may enter.

Protection after Death

My mother translated recently. She was not an ECKist. Does she receive spiritual protection?

You have been going through the most difficult times this past year, but you should know that your mother is spiritually protected and cared for because of your love and service to SUGMAD.

Everything you do is what the ECK is allowing for a greater expression of the Sound and Light to people who do not know about ECK, as well as to those who do.

Express Lane

How soon after the demise of the body can cremation take place? How long does Soul hover near the body before Its journey toward whatever plane is Its destiny?

Cremation may take place anytime after the death of the body. In ECK, the Mahanta is immediately on hand to greet the individual on the other side. It is a joyful occasion.

Soul has no reason to wait around for three days, as is the case for those who must get an audience with the Lords of Karma. An ECKist goes through the express lane because the Mahanta is with him or her. It is a gift of the Master's love.

Ways to Heal Yourself

I used to wake up in a good mood. Now I wake up with negative thoughts. For example, still half-asleep, I will think thoughts like, I'll get cancer. What is causing this? Are negative entities surrounding me?

You feel there are entities surrounding you. This is an intrusion, and they are in violation of the spiritual law. I suggest you call or visit a professional counselor and discuss your problem. Ask if he or she can help you rid yourself of them.

This is often the way Divine Spirit works to bring relief. It can bring a healing through licensed medical practitioners and counselors.

The problem requires you to take a good, close look at yourself. The law is that no one or nothing can harm us unless we let it do so.

Look first at where the attack is coming from, then examine the emotional body to see if a door has not been shut properly. If someone betrays our trust, it is totally our responsibility to slam shut that door against further intrusion. This must be done with more than just the lips, but especially with the heart.

When one betrays our trust and the outcome leaves us a shattered shell, then we have to exert ourselves and fight back with all the ferocity we can muster in the Soul body.

Imagine a heavy door made of the ECK. Put all your strength into swinging it shut. Lock it, bolt it, chain it, and then drop a bar across the door. Turn around and walk farther into the Temple of Golden

35

Wisdom. You are walking toward a room of light. Imagine that the Mahanta is there to meet you.

Put no more thought upon the dark forces of fear that are now locked out.

Protection with HU

Can you explain briefly what the word HU *means and its use as protection in the dream state?*

HU, a sacred name for God, is popular among members of ECKANKAR, especially in Africa. Black magic is a very powerful force there, able to wreak havoc. An ECKist who is the object of a curse sings this word *HU* and also pictures a shield of white light between himself and the black magician.

The white light is the Light of God. HU is the Sound of God. The Light and Sound are the two most trusted pillars of protection that one can ever find.

People in Europe, Australia, and the Americas also sing HU quietly or aloud to receive protection from trouble or danger on the street, at work, or in the home.

HU is a powerful defense.

Becoming a Happier Person

I would like to be happy, but I am often depressed. Can you help?

I received your request for healing, and the matter has been put into the hands of Divine Spirit to do with as It will. As a further suggestion, have you approached professional counseling, besides medical doctors? The Family Service Association is listed in the phone book's white pages in many larger towns.

The reason I offer the suggestion is this: Spirit brings help through a coordination of effort on both the invisible planes as well as the physical. Spiritually, then, the matter is turned over to Divine Spirit. To complete our willingness to do our own part down here, we make appointments with professional counselors who are trained to dislodge entities.

These are only suggestions. In addition, it will be useful to sing HU softly whenever you feel the negative presence. HU is an ancient name for God and sounds like the word *hue,* but in a long, drawn-out, continuing way.

Are You Trapped by Time?

I need your help to break free of a trap I've allowed myself to be in. My husband and I are not together, but he's still supporting me. If I had the strength and stick-to-it powers, I would get a job to support myself. But as hard as I try, I can't push myself to find a job.

Please read *Talons of Time* by Paul Twitchell again, if you will. Pay special attention to the role of the Time Makers and how they trap Soul and introvert It between the start of any action and its goal.

Then let the Inner Master help sweep away the webs that keep Soul in chains. You will have to make the effort, but if you do I can help you via the inner channels.

How HU Can Heal You

I am in desperate need of help. I am totally possessed and controlled by a powerful psychic. This woman feels she owns me—she is actually changing the structure of my brain and my entire personality!

This entity has lodged itself in your consciousness, but there is something which can rid you of it. I suggest you sing the word HU for up to half an hour at a time—but no longer, unless the entity bothers you again. The entity will put up a terrific struggle, but its hold will gradually weaken over a period of several weeks if you sing the word faithfully.

HU, the sacred name for God, opens the channels of healing. This word is empowered to open the door to spiritual healing. Anytime a thought from this entity intrudes upon your mind, sing HU. The entity will repeatedly try to establish itself as a parasite in your consciousness.

It will take diligence to catch its approach and begin the song of HU, which will certainly bring the spiritual travelers of ECK to your aid. The ECK Masters are able to help only if you ask for their aid directly!

Also, I suggest you burn any letters from this person and cut off all outer communication. You should have relief after thirty days. Then be prepared to go to a counseling service and ask for help. That is often the way Divine Spirit chooses to help us out of our emotional and mental entanglements.

The real question is: How did she get such a hold on you? One common problem is that we study too many different spiritual paths at the same time and unwittingly open our psychic centers. Alcohol and drugs can have the same effect.

What the ECK Masters Want for You

I am afraid of working with the ECK Masters because a friend of mine says that some people try to control others in the dream state. Can you tell me the truth about this?

I have no interest in controlling other people, since no spiritual purpose is ever served by that.

The negative force can and does come disguised as me as well as other people. To protect yourself against such deception, sing HU or call upon a spiritual leader you know and trust: the Mahanta, Christ, etc.

My mission is to help true seekers find their way home to God. For this reason, ECK initiates are given wide discretion to run their inner lives.

The path of ECK is not meant to finally end the succession of life's problems, for they are given as opportunities for Soul's unfoldment.

3

Solving Problems

I'm seventy years old, and I've been in ECK several years; but I haven't had what I'd call spiritual experiences. I try to keep my attention on the Tisra Til during my exercises, but after the first five minutes, I can only think of all the things I should be doing. No doubt I am very much in need of God, but I haven't found IT yet. I'm afraid I will not learn what is on the other planes until I die. Can ECKANKAR really help me?

I appreciate your sincere question about the lack of spiritual unfoldment. ECK is an individual path, as is life. I can give you no guarantees about success here or anyplace else. What I can do is share some of the things that worked for me at one time or another.

First, understand that not everyone is conscious of his experiences on the spiritual planes while living in the physical body. The curtain must be drawn across the memory at certain times in order for the ECKist to retain a balance in this physical world. Others are quite aware of the Sound and Light of ECK.

There is a way some may develop their memory of

41

their dreams by keeping a notebook and pen at the bedside. But it takes a remarkable amount of self-discipline to rouse oneself from a deep sleep, turn on the bed lamp, and scrawl down notes for ten to fifteen minutes in a cold room. Not everyone is up to it.

There are times a block in our spiritual lives prevents us from entering the next spiritual plateau. It is possible to do a fast of some sort to remove this block. Not everyone is able to do this, and it should always be done with the advice of a physician.

Here's what I did: When the dream memory stopped for a period of time, new efforts in a new direction were necessary to break through. I would go on a juice fast for a day, then regular food the next day, then juice again for the following day—and alternate between solid food and juices for several days. But I never did it too long at first, since our health is not always able to withstand the strain. This is an individual matter that I cannot recommend unless your doctor says it is all right.

I would also address myself honestly and ask: What do I want out of ECK? Our motives must be pure.

The inner experiences are not to be used to lord our supposed spiritual greatness over others. Nor to brag about them. What do we want these experiences for? Rebazar Tarzs said that experiences are a rupee a dozen.

Quite frankly, not everyone is ready for ECK. That is all right. We are concerned with our personal relationship with the ECK and the SUGMAD. One person may need phenomenal experiences, while another may not. Some ECKists have written that the flashy experiences are not what they want, but merely the seeing, knowing, and being that comes when one enters the Soul Plane and becomes established there.

There were times when it seemed that the Spiritual Exercises of ECK had stopped working for me. Looking back, I realize it was generally for one of two reasons: I had overstepped some spiritual law, such as the Law of Silence, or my spiritual life had entered one of its periodic quiet stages. The conscious and the unconscious states often alternate. When it was quiet I worked on the virtues of patience, for the impatient person certainly will never find God.

If you're able to find any help to break through the spiritual blockage by something written here, I would appreciate hearing from you. It is Divine Spirit that assists us on the inner planes and not the personality of even the Living ECK Master.

I thank you for your concern with this situation and recommend that you experiment freely with the spiritual exercises that are found in the ECK discourses.

Why Do Troubles Come?

Can you explain why we have problems?

Troubles that come to us are for our purification. They come to us because we must learn a divine law.

The ECK will use the most negative situations to teach us, and we wonder, Why has God forsaken me? God has not forsaken us. We are unwilling to give up certain passions of the mind and take the next step in our spiritual development. Habits fall away once Soul decides It really wants spiritual realization more than Its vices.

The path of ECK is not meant to finally end the succession of life's problems, for they are given as opportunities for Soul's unfoldment. What the ECKist does develop, however, is the inner link with the ECK.

43

Thus he taps into the Supreme Creative Force that guides him around all the blocks in his path that once defeated him.

One's ability to take charge of his own life increases. This is a solid step toward self-mastery and that state of consciousness called the kingdom of heaven.

Be Kinder to Yourself

I am going through some hard times, and I feel so alone. I am only fifteen, but I am not sure I want to live here on earth. What's wrong with me?

You are a special person who has a lot to give others, but you've got to learn to be kinder to yourself. There's no school that teaches that, of course, but you can strike an attitude of openness as to how that can come to be.

If you have quiet conversations with yourself, ask, How can I be kinder to myself? Asking will open a door. Watch for people who live a life of kindness to themselves and others. For now, don't try to copy them—just watch.

Believe me, a lot of people much older than you don't know what to do with their lives. But there are people who act with kindness. Watch for them, and you'll find exactly the kind of life you're looking for. But you'll have to work for it. We all pay our dues.

Are You Mixing Two Paths?

I'm having to write you again because I'm having terrible visions. I have talked to my friend, an ECKist, and he has explained to me about the psychic I've been going to. The visions are starting to appear two or three times a night. I'm behind in my sleep and totally dread the evening. Please help me.

The cause of the disturbing visions is that you are mixing the psychic field with the spiritual way of ECK. A terrible storm thus develops within the human consciousness.

The safest thing to do is first get the psychic centers in your body closed. Call a Family Service Association (there's one in the phone book's white pages in larger cities), and ask for advice for your problem. See what counseling can be directed to you and the cost.

If you take the positive step to seek qualified counseling, then Divine Spirit will begin straightening out your spiritual tangle.

Take Care of Yourself First

I have a problem raising enough money to attend ECK seminars. I scraped together enough to attend the last ECK Worldwide Seminar but was overwhelmed by bills when I got home. I'm trying to get control over this situation. Do you have any advice?

It is true that we do not try to solve problems, but rather control them. We truly have a choice in our private lives whether or not to use money for bills or to attend a seminar.

All who attend the ECK seminars with open hearts have the blessings of ECK. Yet there's no reason to create hardships for ourselves. We must use common sense.

Why Troubles Equal Unfoldment

Lately I have been through a very lonely time where sadness has been a frequent visitor. When I realized

45

that the way back to God was mine to travel alone and that I couldn't even talk about some of these things with my husband, the pain was intense.

The troubles we face are only for our own unfoldment. Our trials are difficult for us, but they mean little to our neighbor. He has his own troubles.

The way becomes narrower, but as our self-discipline to do those things that help us along the path increases, we discover that life can no longer defeat us. We move tranquilly under the protection of that Presence we know as the ECK.

Our service to God, then, is given in the little things of life. The joy of spiritual awareness that now lights up our consciousness puts discouragement aside.

Each problem we control makes us greater in the eyes of God and one step closer to self-mastery.

Attitudes Create Your World

Why don't troubles go away once we ask for help?

Much of the trouble we have in life is a result of some long-standing negative attitude. It has created these situations. Soul gains experience as It works through these rough spots on the road.

Some of our troubles will be dispelled by Divine Spirit while others are not. They are part of the divine plan for Soul to gain the purification or change in consciousness so It can know what It is. It needs to know why It has reincarnated into today's family and business environment.

Many people do not understand that life, with its burdens, is a treasure. The weight of disappointment makes us close our eyes to the gift of being in the world to learn about the loving heart.

Rising from Failure

I am depressed over the condition I find my life in. I cannot even look for a job because I am afraid I would just be bored with it, and I am not able to face another failure. What can I do?

Sit down and list the things you like and do not like about yourself, in separate columns. Look at them once a month when you write your initiate report. Look back over the past thirty days for any changes the ECK has brought to you.

Self-discipline is an absolute necessity if one is to have a productive life in ECK. Replace old tastes and preferences with new, better ones. But do it in the name of the ECK, with love and a sincere heart, or nothing will come of this experiment.

You must also look at how you wish to spend your time at work. Plot out a rough plan of getting (and holding) a job that has the things in it needed to keep your interest. Take care of the outer needs of the body because they are important for a sense of well-being. What you want to do is live the complete life in ECK.

The spiritual exercises build up spiritual momentum for Soul to realize the God-like being that It is; therefore, it is imperative that you do them for a twenty-minute period every day. If you have the discipline for that, I will certainly be with you at all times.

Lack of Harmony with Others

What happens when two people get inner guidance in different directions? How can they resolve this, and why did it happen anyway?

There are two answers to this riddle. First, one or the other did not hear the Mahanta correctly. That is usually the case. Second, they both got the Master's message wrong.

The possible remedy is to have a neutral third party help sort out the pieces. Ask to see an ECK Spiritual Aide, who will mostly listen. The Master's real direction often becomes clear during the ESA session.

No two people are alike. Each has an agreement with life that is unlike any other. Learn love, patience, and grace, because they are the way to find harmony.

Finding peace is a big part of your spiritual life.

A friend is always trying to draw me into her conflicts. How do I handle this problem, since she is very close to me?

There are people who try to draw others into their problems. Their own troubles are overwhelming because they like the attention from others.

Of course, how much you choose to become a part of her world is for you to decide. But don't feel guilty if you want to pull out of the situation because it interferes with your life.

She has to make up her own mind about personal decisions. If the Inner Master gives her a direction, fine. I will not intrude upon her consciousness unless she asks.

In short, all her decisions have to be her own. You may act as a listening post if you want to. But don't let her take your life away from you.

How Problems Change as You Grow

As I go along in ECK, my problems seem to get bigger, yet I am able to handle them better. Can you explain this?

As you grow spiritually, you're forced to address problems that the average person wouldn't even dream existed. Once you wade through the cobwebs and dig out a solution, the same kind of problem-solving can be transferred to the next difficulty that comes along. We can learn to be on top of things instead of being the reactive victims.

The only thing that keeps me plugging along in the face of difficult situations is that in the high worlds of ECK there is no time or space. Therefore, our detours are only so much learning. There is no point in getting somewhere faster or slower, sooner or later. SUGMAD cares only that Soul is perfected sometime in Its wanderings. Nobody is in a hurry.

How can anyone get lost in the worlds of ECK? Such a thing is not possible. We've all done our share of racing ahead and sliding back in our lives. After all, that is the way of nature here—a constant back-and-forth motion that ends in maturity.

Doing Things That Frighten Us

Last month I was supposed to give an introductory ECK talk, but I panicked and left before anyone arrived. Three miles down the freeway I turned back, but the ECK had already brought another chela who thought it was her week to give the talk. I need some help in facing this stage fright.

Don't feel like a misplaced person because you suffer from stage fright. A survey I recently read said that the number one fear for most people is the thought of giving a talk before an audience. You did have the courage to return to the ECK Center to give the intro talk if you had to, even though the ECK had brought someone else there to do it instead.

There are two approaches to doing things that frighten us: face them, or arrange our lives so that particular fear is moved out of our lives. I think the second way is kinder to ourselves.

If the ECK wants you to serve as a public speaker anyway, It will move you into public speaking in such a way that you experience the least discomfort.

So for now, if stage fright is making your life a terror, ask to serve in a way more suited to your temperament. The Master wants each individual to eventually go beyond the small self and become a greater being in Spirit.

Soul's Love for God

What really causes all the problems I have in my life?

This connection may or may not make sense to you, but many of the things that have caused you problems are Soul's desire to love God.

When one feels unable to receive such love, life is meaningless. I wish I had words to say this better.

When you ask for help, the ECK begins to bring changes that are for your good. Of course, this means you must be extra careful in the choices you make. Before ECK can make any changes, you must develop a better image of yourself: You are Soul. God's love is for you.

The Road to God

My life is filled with money problems and other kinds too many to enumerate. I am asking you for guidance so I can go on. I want to understand how to solve these problems. I also want to gain the under-standing to allow the ECK to really express Itself in my life.

All problems come from the inner to the outer; therefore, we want to find out what is being done on the inner planes that is bringing about the problems out here, which seem to be too much to endure at times.

There is no need to run through clichés such as "There is no such thing as an accident," "All that befalls us is for a reason," or similar sayings. But what is causing all the trouble in terms that can be understood and accepted? And what is the solution?

The individual must be honest with himself and ask, What did I expect from ECK when I took up the teachings? The path to God is the path to God. It is not an easy one, otherwise many would be on it.

Life is truly meeting ourselves. The complaints we have of others are reflections of our own deficiencies. It makes no sense to patch up our spiritual life with Band-Aids. The teachings of ECK are to give us a deep spiritual healing that touches all aspects of our lives. It's not done with a magic wand, however. Has one kept up the spiritual exercises, not with the robotic diligence of a person using prayer beads, but with a real desire to open himself to the secrets of God?

There are two basic paths for one to take in the lower worlds in an effort to find God—the path of love or the path of power. Most opt for power. This direction is the breeding ground for all the ills that come from the five passions of the mind. Life is for him a disaster, and he wonders what keeps him from taking an easy way out.

Love is the only way to the SUGMAD. The only way. If you want to go this route, ask the Mahanta in

51

contemplation to be shown the way. Most people in ECK have not found it. Otherwise there would be less gossip coming from their lips, less complaints, less power plays in the ECK Center.

The individual's heart must be pure in this request to be shown the way. There must also be a complete surrender to the Inner Master, no holding back or having opinions of what is right or wrong about what is given him to light the Golden Heart. The ECK is real but Its altar must be come to with humility and love, if one is to ever see Its ways.

One is no longer at the mercy of destiny and the blind fates but becomes a knowing being who understands the secret laws that govern his affairs. He is like the sailor who knows the ocean currents; he can chart a course to a destination and be quite certain of getting there in his sailboat.

4

Past Lives and the ECK-Vidya

*A new ability has come to me—that of prophecy.
I have been able to foresee events in my own life
and those of others. But I feel this is also a spiritual
test. Can you help me understand the hidden dangers
of this gift?*

I received your recent letter about your consciousness being opened to prophecy. There is a test that
goes along with this. It can be overlooked by the one
who is given the ability. The test is: What will you do
with it?

Prophecy is not to be done for or about another
person, without permission. People who do so want
power over such an individual. This is a misuse of the
God power. There is quite a punishment exacted for
such a flagrant violation of the spiritual law.

Thus the paradox is that one who gets the gift of
prophecy is not able to tell anyone about it. He must
follow the Law of Silence. Otherwise, the road to
unfoldment stops right there.

Others have gone through this test successfully
before; some have failed it. You are also at the crossroads. The choice is up to you.

I do not allow anyone on the path of ECK to misuse the ECK power to make themselves important in their own eyes or in the eyes of others. The Co-workers with God work quietly, effectively, and humbly. Their only wish is to carry the seed of the ECK message to every corner of their community in a dignified manner, with common sense.

No one, in fact, knows who most of these mysterious spiritual workers are because of the quiet way they serve the SUGMAD.

Past-Life Study Tips

Please share some simple ways to open past lives for study.

I prefer that ECKists trace their past lives through their study of dreams. There are many reasons for this that time does not allow me to go into here.

To awaken such past-life dreams, make a note of things you greatly like or dislike. Do that also with people. Then watch your dreams. Also note if a certain country or century attracts you. There is a reason.

How to Unwind Your Karma

My husband left me suddenly almost five years ago, and I cannot get my life nor my finances straightened out. After reading many books I was beginning to develop psychic abilities, but then they stopped. Please check my Akashic record to see why these things are happening.

While the past records of anyone's life are important in determining certain causes and effects in his life, most of the problems that arise from the past cannot be solved simply by a knowledge of it. Otherwise most psychic readers who are good at reading the Akashic records would be able to help people straighten out unhappy lives at will.

But this does not happen. Somebody must have the knowledge of how to begin unwinding the intricate karma that has brought one to the present-day trouble. This is a spiritual skill that is known to very few of those who can read the past records.

The Adepts in ECK have a single purpose in mind when a seeker comes to them for relief: to give that Soul the opportunity for achieving wisdom, power, and freedom, three attributes of God-Realization. This means simply that an individual learns to be like the Adepts, enjoying a 360-degree viewpoint, the center of which is a love for all living things.

When one gains even a degree of this love, he is himself able to restructure his life along lines that suit him. He is no longer at the mercy of destiny and the blind fates, but becomes a knowing being who understands the secret laws that govern his affairs. He is like the sailor who knows the ocean currents; he can chart a course to a destination and be quite certain of getting there in his sailboat.

Most of the cause for your present trouble is indeed from the past, but not in the desertion of your mate then or now. There is a tendency for you to lean upon others, to let them think for you. When this rubber crutch is leaned upon, it gives way and you fall down, at the mercy of every sort of misfortune that can be imagined. Therefore, the lesson that Soul must learn in this case is to find a more substantial inner support than It has in the past.

Your problems with failing finances are simply due to a lack of knowledge about the ins and outs of finance. I suggest you make an effort to learn about the financial areas that would be most helpful to you in the immediate future. If you let go and give your concerns to Divine Spirit, you will be guided to the best avenue to take next. Look over all the different ways open to you to learn about finance: local courses in the community, help from a friend who is well off in money matters, or books in the library.

There is no more magic about setting one's self up financially than there is for an experienced cook to bake a cake. There is a recipe for success no matter what field one is in. Failure, like a fallen angel-food cake, means the cook overlooked something important in the baking process that a better cook does by second nature.

Too many people want to use the psychic field as a shortcut to improving their lives. They feel there is a magical route that will leapfrog them over the hardship of self-discipline. The psychic field is set in an unstable force and will fail just as a person thinks he has a certain method for predicting the future down pat.

In ECK, I want to show people how to become open channels for Divine Spirit. Remember, Soul has come into the lower worlds in many different incarnations in order to learn to be a Co-worker with God. A mechanical method of restructuring your life will fail unless there is also an upliftment in consciousness. I recommend you read *The Golden Heart*. In it is a simple spiritual exercise called "The Easy Way." It is one way of opening oneself to the more bountiful life of Spirit.

Time Twins

What is meant by the term spiritual twin *as mentioned in* The ECK-Vidya, Ancient Science of

58

Prophecy? *Does it have to do with past lives?*

It does not refer to Soul mates, or time twins.

The old idea rests upon a lesser line of affinity that can exist between two people. It may include such things as physical appearance, a common interest in a social cause, or even a chemical bond between two people.

These values are of Kal, or negative in nature.

Spiritual twins are something else. They are two people who each want the ECK more than anything else in life. And they help each other reach It. In time, the male and female forces within each come into harmony, as they reach the Soul Plane and become the ECK Itself.

That is love at its finest.

Can You See Past Lives?

I would like to see my past lives. How do I go about this?

When we practice the Spiritual Exercises of ECK faithfully, the Inner Master will open us up to those things that are important to see concerning past lives. Most of them need not concern us. No matter what we were in the past during any other life, we are spiritually greater today.

The wealth and position we enjoyed in past lives mean nothing unless we know how to lift ourselves from materialism into the higher worlds. This does not mean to shun the good things of this life—family, home, wealth. God loves the rich man as much as the poor. We get no special benefits if we fall for the negative tricks of asceticism or unusual austerities.

We live the spiritual life beginning where we are

today. We look to see the hand of Divine Spirit guiding us toward the greater consciousness, which leads us to becoming a more direct vehicle for Spirit.

Friends from the Past

In my dreams, I am often with friends from the past whom I no longer see in the physical. These people had a big influence in my life at one time, but why are they in my dreams so often today?

Your question deals with the very broad sweep of reincarnation. The family you live with today is only a small part of the extended family from your past.

Each person's past link with other people in this life is more like being a member of a far-flung clan, which goes well beyond the close members of today's family. So in this life, other members of your extended family come as schoolmates, friends of childhood, teachers, and the like.

They remain in your dreams because they are a very real part of you. For this lifetime, though, they have chosen a different mission and life-style, so you go along your separate paths.

But your inner bond spans time.

Reading the ECK-Vidya

I am about to move myself and my business to another state. I would like to make this move with more light and clarity. How can I get an ECK-Vidya reading from you?

I appreciate your letter and request for an ECK-Vidya reading. My schedule is such that I do not read these anymore. The ECKist is encouraged to develop the ability to read the ECK-Vidya for himself through the Spiritual Exercises of ECK. The key for learning about one's past, present, and future can be gotten through a study of it.

There comes a time when one learns about the ECK-Vidya as a step in unfoldment, but there is also a time when the ECKist puts it aside in his striving for God-Realization.

I am very interested in developing an ability to read the ECK-Vidya. How can I learn more about this ancient art?

The whole thing is more than just a study program; it's an in-depth cleansing. That's why there aren't a lot of ECK-Vidya readers. The rugged discipline it requires goes over the heads of most people. A trust between you and the ECK begins to form like an object out of thin air.

The ECK-Vidya reading is but half done when the reader receives it. He must, in turn, make a full study of it, take it into contemplation nightly to the Mahanta. It must be a union of both the exoteric and the esoteric knowledge.

Gradually, the ECK-Vidya reading is found to be less the single, flawless, unimpeachable word on the matter, but a starting place for the expansion of consciousness in the one who receives it.

Healing the Past through Dreams

How can one heal oneself in the dream state?

It is possible to get a healing for many conditions, like poor health, emotions, or mental stress. But not always. The study of dreams in ECKANKAR begins with the fact of past lives. All conditions are due to karma, and some will last a lifetime, such as the loss of a limb. A study of dreams can help people learn the spiritual reason their life is as it is, and what they can do to improve their lot.

A way to heal oneself begins with a spiritual exercise. At bedtime, sing the word HU. Softly sing this ancient name for God for five to ten minutes. Also create a mental picture of your problem. See it as a simple cartoon. Beside it, place another image of the condition as you feel it should be.

The second week, if you've had no luck seeing a past life, do this dream exercise for fifteen or twenty minutes. Take a rest the third week. Repeat this cycle until you succeed.

Keep a record of your dreams. Make a short note about every dream you recall upon awakening. Also be alert during the day for clues about your problem from other people. The Holy Spirit works through them too.

So be aware and listen.

Reasons for Loneliness

I am beset by a terrible loneliness at times but am at a loss to explain it. I am an isolated person—not that I want to be; it just seems to always work out that way. This has been with family, friends, and mates, as well as jobs and people connected to them. Everything is very short-lived, and it doesn't seem normal. I do the best I can, but no matter what I do things are always interrupted and ending all the time.

As far back as I can remember, it has always been this way. Whatever is going on I know has to do with some past life I lived.

I greatly appreciated your letter and will try to shed some light on the feelings of loneliness you spoke of.

Most of the karma we make is from this lifetime, although periodically there is a long-standing condition hanging on from another lifetime.

Imagine, if you will, the life of a leper in Palestine shortly before the Christian era. Anyone with a diagnosis of leprosy faced a life of separation from his family and friends. The repeated reactions of horror and disgust by citizens when coming across lepers would be enough to leave a deep scar for centuries.

Anyone who reincarnates into the present life from such an existence ought to look on the positive side. What a blessing to no longer be regarded as a scourge among people because of a disfiguring disease! Just this thought alone ought to make one appreciate a healthier body in this lifetime.

Do the Spiritual Exercises of ECK, and I, as the Inner Master, will work with you.

Claims by Others

I've come across claims by two people who say they are from other planets. What does this mean?

People who just haven't gotten recognition in this lifetime often pretend to be reincarnations of royalty, visitors from space, or some other noble being that puts them above their fellows.

Of course, their past is always of the kind that cannot be checked out by somebody else. Who can go to ancient Egypt and verify that someone was a queen in several centuries B.C.? All that one can do is take these claims upon the authority of the person who makes them, which is a rather doubtful position to be in. Usually these people are harmless and never get more than a ripple of attention from anybody—certainly not from crowds.

One is judged by what he does rather than what he claims to be.

Someone I recently met has given me information I don't know what to do with. She says that I was a famous musician, she a famous writer—that we have been together before. I am frightened out of my mind. She says we have karma together, and it is my fear that we must marry even though I don't even want a relationship with this person. I need your help badly.

I appreciate your letter and questions about your past lives. It should relieve you to learn that you were not the person she claims you were.

It is your decision how you will use this information in your personal affairs with the other individual. This can be taken to the inner through the Spiritual Exercises of ECK. That will give you a direction in some manner, whether subtle or direct.

Past-Life Readings

I've become very interested in past-life regression and am considering getting training in this area. My concern is: Do I have to give up my ECKANKAR membership totally, or can I continue with the understanding that this service would in no way be affiliated with ECKANKAR? I feel that it would be a valuable service in our medicine fields and would appreciate your guidance in this matter.

You have the freedom to conduct your private life in whatever way you must. I do ask, though, as you have already stated, that this service be in no way affiliated with ECKANKAR. This includes not leaking word to ECKists through the grapevine that you are available for this service.

The reason is that past-life memory can seriously injure someone if the past is opened without competent guidance. Usually it creates additional deep-seated problems worse than those that led him to seek such help.

The Inner Master gives whatever snatches of the past are important and when the person is emotionally strong enough to take it. That is generally at a very slow, measured pace.

The tangles of past karma are tied in with the memories of past-life experiences and must be dealt with so carefully. The hypnotist often lacks the spiritual training to deal with karma and pass it off into the Audible Life Stream. That's also one reason, in a parallel case, that the suicide rate among psychiatrists is so great.

Local chelas in our area are very enthused about past-life readings. I am very concerned about this. Is there any benefit to these readings for the chelas?

Some people need that sort of service until they go beyond that level. The ECK Masters must make bridges for people from their states of consciousness.

Many who are going to readers now will grow into higher understandings of ECK. Then they will not need the rubber crutch provided by past-life readers.

I am open now to new ways to bring the Sound and Light to those who are ready for it. People at all levels of life can find their niche in ECK, but we must provide a bridge.

For some, the bridge of interest is past-life readings. I started there. People outgrow their childhood, but if that's where they are now, that's where we must meet them.

The path of ECK is not for the God-Realized but for those who wish to reach that station—no matter what their starting point.

The past is past. It holds nothing more for the seeker of God, for he practices the spiritual exercises and lives in the Sound and Light of Divine Spirit.

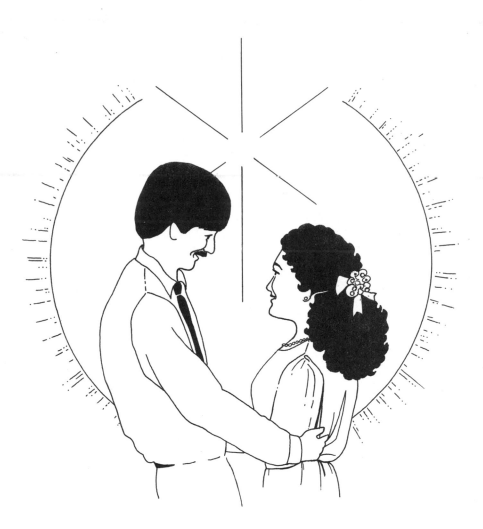

A true marriage has commitment by each person. Both realize the responsibility of that commitment. A marriage of the heart lets each of the couple remain an individual, but the two are as one.

5

Family Relationships

*W**hat does the marriage bond signify spiritually?*
Why can married couples share their initiations
and secret words?

The marriage bond can only be sacred if it is
sacred to the two individuals who have agreed to this
union. If they are one in heart, how can they be
divided? At their marriage, one ECK couple made a
"first cause" statement to each other. They each made
a vow to help the other become a Vairagi Master in
this lifetime. They would help each other in conscious
spiritual evolution, out of love, to reach the heights of
God.

A true marriage has commitment by each person.
Both realize the responsibility of that commitment. A
marriage of the heart lets each of the couple remain
an individual, but the two are as one.

Their close spiritual bond often lets them
share initiations and secret words. But the ECK
initiation always comes as a result of one's personal
unfoldment.

Finding True Love

My husband isn't an ECKist per se, but he evidently learned a great deal about contemplation early in life. Our beliefs seem different, but they aren't really. He isn't well physically, and we both know his time is short. I want to know if he is all right not being an ECKist on the outer.

Life indeed leads us down unexpected but interesting trails. One such trail was the one that brought you and your husband together. The joy of a spiritual bond such as yours will continue beyond this life.

Your life with your husband has shown so clearly that not all ECKists are in ECK. In fact, it's not even possible, in fairness, to create such categories of consciousness. Either one knows the Spirit of Love or he doesn't.

The same rule applies to ECKists too. Those who have the love of God within them belong to a spiritual race of advanced beings. Outwardly they may look no different from their neighbors, but they are carriers of the Light and Sound of God—even though not always conscious of it.

Responsibilities to Your Family

I am Japanese, and my husband is an American. My husband has been reading books about how the world is going to end in 1999. He wants to go to a community in Arkansas and grow crops. This would mean leaving me and our baby son in Japan, but he doesn't seem to care. Do you encourage people to leave their family if they want to?

For centuries people have predicted the end of the world. Needless to say, they've been wrong. The same

70

doubts troubled people in the years shortly before A.D. 1000 as trouble others as we approach A.D. 2000. Such a prediction is not part of the ECK teachings.

The world will continue for many thousand more years. Therefore, there is no need for your husband to run off to another part of the world "to do good."

In ECK we know that our responsibility is first toward ourselves and our families. How can anyone expect to help others if he abandons his own family?

In ECKANKAR, as in any group, you will find people who are highly responsible as well as those who are not. Those who are not responsible to their own cause them much needless sorrow.

I find myself still aspiring to physical things, for example, the construction of my home. Being a new ECKist, this has confused me. On one hand I am afraid that this is a negative attachment to material things; while at the same time, I feel I am merely fulfilling my responsibilities to my family.

I am grateful for your letter. Please know that one must provide for his family as well as possible. That has nothing to do with attachment. The ECK Masters do not want anyone to live in poverty or give up house, family, or possessions.

God loves Soul rich or poor. God does not necessarily love the poor more. God loves Soul. Thus we can enjoy the things of this life and support our family with material goods with no feelings of guilt.

The path of ECK is merely to open our consciousness so that we can become greater vehicles for Divine Spirit. Thus ECK enhances our life and gives insight, strength, and understanding where we found only darkness before.

When to Share with a Mate

Do I have to keep the Law of Silence with my husband about an inner experience that included him?

There are no secrets between a couple in ECK. Does this mean we want to tell all our secrets all the time?

If your husband is with you on the inner planes, you may tell him about it in the morning. Afterward check your inner bodies to see whether you are still filled with the lightness and spaciousness that came with it, or are you left empty?

Talking does slow experiences down. This is not all bad, especially when inner events have sped up so fast that we wonder how much longer we can possibly hang on. Talk to your mate, but do not tell the general public.

Staying Free through Charity

Does sympathy for a friend cause a transfer of karma?

You'll never pick up karma from a friend's misfortune as long as you conduct yourself with true love. This is a pure love that does not try to change conditions. This same love is called charity. It simply loves those whom it loves and is willing to leave it at that. Any healing that might occur is up to the ECK.

Two Paths, One Marriage

When I first sent for my ECK discourses, my husband was quite agreeable. But after learning more about it, he is very much against ECKANKAR. I am not permitted to do my spiritual exercises or attend

72

*classes. I have been suffering severe illnesses and am
in need of your advice.*

Concerning situations where the ECK teachings
bring a reaction in the home, it is better to step back
from the outer works and continue quietly by yourself
until matters improve.

You will continue to receive the love and protection
of Divine Spirit in spiritual matters as long as you
want them. I would rather see harmony in the home
than have a family torn apart by differences of belief.

Much of the illness is due to the disharmonies that
swirl about you, the fears and anxieties. For this I
suggest the continued help of the medical profession,
for Spirit frequently uses that means to bring physical
relief.

Divine Spirit tends to hold families together whenever possible. I do not want a husband and wife to
fight over their different religious beliefs. Harmony in
a family is a sacred thing.

When Your Family Is Hurting

*Members of my husband's family have been very
upset with us since we joined ECKANKAR. Since my
Second Initiation I have felt awful. I have tried contemplation, but only thoughts of anger come to mind.
I've gotten some therapy to overcome these low moods.
What can I do to help myself and my family through
this?*

It is good you are getting professional help to
overcome the negative feelings that are affecting your
family.

To help with your therapy, consider stepping back
from the outer works of ECK until you can turn the

corner with the personal concerns that are overwhelming you. The crosscurrents are too strong right now between your personal problems and trying to be active with the outer ECK works. This is up to you of course. You still have the love and protection of the Mahanta.

The turmoil in your family is a difficult time for all of you. It seems as though the lines are drawn as sharply as they were in the Civil War, when brother turned against brother for an ideal. All of it is needed for your spiritual enrichment, odd as that might seem from your vantage point in the midst of the hurricane.

At first glance, it seems an unfortunate thing to be in such difficulty, but the ECK always has some purpose, even in the most extreme situations. It is not the hard knocks in our lives that are of any real importance, but what we do when they hit us. The attitude is the measure.

I had a divorce that I am unhappy about. I have four children; two live with their dad. This situation makes me very unhappy. Do you think it is too late to somehow gather all my family back together?

You might start by taking soundings of how each person you wish to be with again feels about it. A lot of pain occurs on all sides in a marital separation, and it doesn't go away overnight. Besides, as time passes, each of your family has gotten older and has begun to fashion a new life for themselves.

Parents who stay together in their marriage see the growing independence of their children on a day-to-day basis. But in a separation, the parents whose children live away may not be able to keep up emotionally with the growing independence of their children.

Growth and change are natural parts of living. We

74

are unhappy when, for some reason, we cannot keep up with them.

So, you must look first at yourself with complete honesty. Do this by taking a sharp look at all the people in your dreams of a family as of old. Look at each person honestly. How old were they when they left? How old are they now? What interests did they have then? Now? The hard part, if there is to be one, is the condition of how things are *now.*

People respond quicker to warm interest and love than to criticism. When hurt and misunderstandings occur in a marital split-up, the old fears do not dissolve overnight. Indeed, they may never go away.

There are a minimum of two parties in a relationship. It takes the cooperation of both if it is to continue. If you're the willing party and the other side is not, there is little to be done to nurture such a relationship. Go on with your life.

Life isn't run by people who are experts in living. Neither are marriages. We're all beginners for the most part, doing the best we can. This means making mistakes of all kinds, of all degrees. Some can be righted by apologies or forgiveness, but many others cannot: Only time can be the healer, and not always in this lifetime.

You've got to look at yourself first, with sincerity and love. The past is past. It may not be fully in your hands to build a new future like the past. But you will be able to get a handle on your problem if you start with yourself. Be gentle and kind to yourself. We are all beginners in living.

How Does ECKANKAR View Sex?

What is the connection between ECKANKAR and sex?

75

The search for a Soul mate is an outmoded occult concept. *The Tiger's Fang* tells how the positive and negative currents come together for balance within us. This is Self-Realization.

The deep relationship between man and woman is a sacred token of human love. The sex urge does not lift anyone into the Soul Plane, so why endorse sex as a means for spiritual unfoldment?

This relationship between a couple must be open and clean, without guilt or shame. If you cannot love your family, how will you then love God? The dirt and guilt that the orthodox religions put upon lovemaking is for control of the followers. Guilt and fear have been deeply impressed upon them for centuries.

Lovemaking, a deep expression of love and warmth between a man and woman, is their private business. Overindulgence in anything is lust. Will we be pulled down to the common level of the animal?

The union between man and woman demands mutual responsibility. The ECK Masters advocate virginity until marriage, but I do not intrude into your private life to judge your personal relationships.

Dialogues with the Master, chapter 18, puts more light on the union between man and woman.

Why Virginity until Marriage?

In a past issue of the Letter of Light, *you stated that while it is up to the individual, the ECK Masters advocate chastity or virginity until marriage. Can you please explain why such a life is suggested?*

How can a child raise a child?

People of every society have rules of conduct. These rules say what is right or wrong in that society. Men, women, and children are to obey its rules for the sake of order. The ECK Masters uphold all just laws.

Let's look at a child in society. The child must first learn to care for itself. Today, that often means learning to read and write, do simple chores, make meals, and to clean up after oneself. Later, it also means finding a job.

A baby starts life with no skills at all. It begins to pick up some easy skills as a child. The harder ones come later when it is a young adult. The harder skills are learning to get along with others, even when you don't get your way.

Being born means having to learn to care for ourselves in a society. Each of us must learn how.

But could a ten-year-old girl raise a baby in most parts of the world? I think not, because the girl is herself a child. At what age would she be a good mother? And when does a boy become a man, fit for the duties of being a father? Is it ten, fifteen, or what? Each society has its own rules about that.

So your question is really about being a mature person in society.

When Your Children Are Hurting

My son is a very sensitive child; I guess it is difficult for him to live and function on this plane. School is very stressful for him. He has left his physical body before. The first time we kept him at home, and he came back. This is the second time, and he is in the hospital. How can I help him?

Your son is indeed a wise person in a little boy's body. The experience of thoughtless and cruel children at his school is not in his previous experience, nor to his liking because it is so senseless. Nevertheless, if

77

he could be made to understand the rich opportunity he has as Soul in a human body, he might be able to face the stress. But he needs help, since he's not able to help himself in important areas.

Could the doctors recommend a different school that would have a more restful atmosphere? If your son will talk about it, ask him if he would like to go to another school. He is too sensitive for the give and take found at a regular school.

Remember that your son as Soul will and must finally decide what he wants out of this life, if anything.

Please help me understand why my children were born with so many physical problems. I love them dearly, but it saddens me and is a great strain on my marriage. Is it a strong karmic pattern we will have to live with for a long time?

When we are in the lifetime where we may reach into the higher states of consciousness, past bonds of love are brought into the present so we can resolve them. The greatest thing we can possibly gain from this life is the ability to love, and to love greatly. The ECK brings to us whatever we need and, especially, those who need us and whom we need to fulfill our goal of reaching the richness of love.

Your children have come to you because of your great capacity to give love. And as you can give love, it increases in you. Few will understand the ECK's way of joining you with the richness of love. But in love is life.

You will find *Stranger by the River* to be one of your most beautiful companions. No matter what comes, remember that the Mahanta is with you in everything. He is giving you the love so you can give it to your own.

78

My son is constantly in a terrible financial bind. Things go well for him for a while, then the bottom drops out. He has a wife and three sons. I supported him for a while after his first marriage, but that didn't work out either. Maternal love is one of the biggest traps of the Kal power. My nature is to leap in to help, but I am trying to see what the lesson is in all of this.

It's hard to be a parent and let our grown-up children learn the consequences of their own actions. We help as long as they learn and it helps them move forward. But there comes a time when we must look out for our own welfare. Who will look out for us when we are unable to do it ourselves?

It's time you took care of your own needs, because it's unlikely that your children will be able to help you.

We love them as much as ever. But they also must learn something: life gives us everything we need, but we must learn to accept its gifts and not turn them away.

Your Children's Experiences

I encourage my child to share his dreams and experiences with me, if he wants to, because I want to help him understand the spiritual side of his life. However, lately I wonder if I should ask him to be silent about his experiences and establish inner discipline.

Talk with him, if he wants to talk. This sets a pattern for him to rely on the inner dreams and remember them.

When a Loved One Dies

My husband translated suddenly while I was away at work. It was a great shock to me, and I feel terrible

*that I was not there when he went. Can you help me
understand why this happened?*

Your husband had finished learning what he had
set out to learn in this lifetime. All the struggles within
him to understand how he stood with the SUGMAD,
the ECK, and the Mahanta are resolved. It's his choice
whether to serve the SUGMAD on the higher planes,
or to return to earth at a later time. For the time being
he is quite satisfied on the Soul Plane, for there are
many regions left to explore there.

It will be possible to meet with him via the dream
state or Soul Travel if you have a strong desire to do
so.

Please do not feel guilty that you were not at home
during his translation. It was the way he wanted it,
to spare you from things he knew at the end, but which
would not have been possible to explain to another. He
is happy.

You will miss him, of course, because the absence
of loved ones in the physical leaves one empty at first.
But in six months you will look back at yourself and
be surprised at how well you have adjusted to this very
great change in your life.

*My daughter was killed in a car accident. The
roads were slick and she was driving fast, when her
car went off a bridge. Thank you for being with her at
the time she made the translation. It has not been easy
for me, for we were so very close, but it would be
impossible without the ECK.*

Even though we are in ECK and clearly know that
Soul lives always, we still miss those close to us when
they leave.

Your daughter, in the Soul state, chose to end this

80

chapter of life in order to begin one that offered her more opportunity for God Consciousness. The one trait she had that matters more than anything is love. Her love for life is so great that she needed more room to express it as a channel for ECK.

You also know that she continues to live and love in the other worlds. It is always possible for you to meet her when the occasion is right. The affinity between you will remain strong because your love for the SUGMAD is strong. Her new life will offer her opportunities that will be a joy for her to learn.

My husband whom I love dearly translated yester-day. He had cancer, but I don't believe he suffered much pain at the end. I know you were there with him. He had wanted very strongly to talk with you by telephone several days ago, but when we called the office, you were not there. I wrote you, but perhaps you didn't get the letter in time. That is my only regret, that he did not get to speak with you.

Your husband is in good hands, and you will be able to meet each other in the dream state, so you both have time to adjust to the idea of his translation from the body.

A letter from me would have made these events stretch out over several more months, giving him false hopes of recovery. He'd completed the spiritual growth he'd come to earth to do, and Soul heard the call of ECK and was ready for new shores.

Love transcends all borders. Your love for each other will endure. The point is that you must now let yourself heal. Crying is a good physician. Please look for me on the inner planes for comfort—that is, look to the Mahanta, which is the spiritual part of myself.

81

The tenderness of your love for each other will remain after the sorrow is gone. By all means, keep your love moving out to others; do not become introverted.

Why do our loved ones have to die? I feel so angry at God.

The passing of a loved one may be a time of sorrow, when we are apt to say, "Dear God, why my beloved?" We understand the order of life, which requires all people to pass to a higher place of existence. But when a loved one goes, we just don't understand.

Impatience and anger will no more bring our loved ones back to us than would patience or love, but these last two qualities can bring us healing.

The Truth about Twins

I would like to know about twins. Are they two Souls or only one?

They are two Souls occupying two bodies. Soul cannot be split or divided. It is a complete unit of God.

Anger in Families

I argue all the time with myself and my family. I've tried exercises and positive thoughts, but I keep on arguing anyway. What should I do?

We get into arguments because we don't like the rules put on us. We feel that somebody has put us in a prison and there is no way out.

The ECK has you in your family because it is the best place for you to learn the customs of society. This sort of discipline gets you ready for the next level of growth and freedom. The ECK won't let us take short-cuts if it would hurt us. We get just the right experience, and not a bit more.

To get in control of your anger, try to catch yourself in the middle of an argument. Then chant HU softly to yourself. Let the argument run its natural course, just to see what it does to you. Suddenly you are surprised to find you are now in control of whether to argue or not, instead of being a helpless victim of your mind. Try this, and see how it works.

Helping Others in Your Family

My sister is always being teased in school. Whenever she tells me and my mother about it, I get an inner nudge to say something to help her feel better. But I can never think of anything to say. Do you know of something I can say or do?

There are two reasons people tease each other: they either like someone or they don't. A boy may tease a girl because he likes her. It's a way he gets her to notice him. If this is what's happening to your sister, just say, "Aw, it's because he likes you." A girl may also cause others to tease her. What's your sister doing to get teased?

Sometimes classmates tease somebody who gets angry over nothing. They try to get an angry person mad. All you can tell her then is this, "Stop getting mad, and they won't have anything to tease you about." Sometimes a child is teased because others are jealous of him or her. This often happens to a child who is very smart or pretty. Then the best thing to do is to smile and try to make a light joke of it. But don't get angry. That just makes it worse. Tell your sister, "Think of

Wah Z. He is always with you. Think of his love for you. Then their teasing can't hurt you."

Can You Love Your Family Too Much?

What is homesickness? Why do some people have it, and others not?

Homesickness hits those who love too much. It is really attachment, a too-strong bond to family and friends while separated from them. It strikes people who are overly loyal, some idealists, and homebodies. There is nothing bad about homesickness, but when a mental passion like that causes misery, the individual would be better off reconsidering his values. Human, never divine, love accounts for homesickness.

What hides behind attachment? The fear of loss. What can overcome such fear? Divine love. And how to find it? In *Stranger by the River,* Rebazar Tarzs discloses the secret: "Open thine eyes, O man, and look steadily for love."

Before you can improve your life and find a measure of happiness, you must learn to do one thing every day out of pure love.

6

Balance and Harmony

I'*ve been an ECKist since early 1973. In 1975, I got myself in a very unbalanced situation where I thought I was losing my mind. I lost my job and my wife, and my whole world crumbled because of this. Somehow I had drastically thrown my emotions out of balance. Although the pain has healed, I am still very much blocked up inside. I ask you with all my heart: Is there some way out of this condition for me?*

I greatly appreciate the concern you expressed about your spiritual life. The question is really, How do I open myself to life and still stay in balance?

Frequently, when one inadvertently opens himself to the spiritual forces before the proper preparation has been made, there is a great series of upsets in personal affairs. This could have been avoided had one known earlier to go slow on any spiritual path: avoid reading too many spiritual books or spending too much time in contemplation.

This is not a criticism, for most of us at one time or another have found ourselves in the same predicament.

The first step to rebuilding our inner worlds is to put some attention here on the physical state of our personal life. Get our business straightened out. Get it together down here on earth. Then gradually and cautiously move out again into those areas of the spiritual things we did not fully understand before and met with in a collision.

You may chant HU for twenty minutes a day—or even Wah Z, which is my spiritual name. But by all means, I urge you to go slowly. If at any time you feel uncomfortable, stop all the spiritual exercises and reading of the ECK works until you feel balanced again.

Sometimes, surprisingly, one's nutrition is lacking. This is often best approached through help with a competent, licensed medical doctor.

Take it easy and don't rush. Guidance can be found inside yourself. It will often come with a gentle nudge to perhaps seek out a doctor or a certain book that is beneficial to you at that particular time.

Why Is Your Life Hard?

I would like to find some love and happiness in my life. But I am in such a muddled state of confusion that I feel I can't get out. I am absolutely broke and exhausted, out of energy to keep going. What am I missing?

Sometimes our life is hard because we make the wrong decisions. Why do we do that? Is it because we're afraid of something? Whatever the reason, this failure has been with us for years.

The teachings of ECK are about us being willing to change our state of consciousness to something better. Unless we agree to such changes, as offered by the

Holy Spirit, they won't come. In fact, they cannot come. Ever.

Ninety-five percent of the ECKists are good people, spiritually in balance. That's not to say they don't have problems, because everyone on earth has problems. But these people do what they can to create a better life for themselves and their loved ones.

The key words here are *loved ones*. One must be able to love in order to have loved ones. Does anyone have a magic wand that can give love to a closed heart? I don't think so. Hearts are open for a reason, and closed hearts are closed for a reason. They don't just happen. Their owners must take responsibility for them, whether they are open or closed. Who else can be responsible if not the owner?

When you're making a decision about something, look at more than the benefits you'll get by doing it, whatever it is. Also look at what price it requires of you. Weigh *both* the benefits and the price before you decide whether to act or not.

Before you can improve your life and find a measure of happiness, you must learn to do one thing every day out of pure love. That means, don't expect anything in return—neither thanks nor happiness. Pick that occasion carefully. Then, whatever that one act of giving of yourself to someone else is, do it with all your heart.

You need to learn to give, without ever thinking of a reward. That's how to find the treasures of heaven.

An ECK Secret

What's the secret of staying in balance?

The secret of a balanced life is to live each moment in the right spiritual frame of mind.

When something appears to go wrong, look for the lesson in it for you, instead of finding fault with anyone else or even yourself.

Inner Harmony

I am very interested in a book by Whitley Strieber called Communion *and enclose a copy for you. In reading this and other books like it, I am concerned about keeping in balance. Is reading books such as this a sidetrack to ECK?*

I would very much like to thank you for sending me *Communion* by Whitley Strieber. It is an area of great interest for a good many people. So little is generally known about alternate states of consciousness as they show up in other beings that inhabit our universe.

An interest such as this can become an all-consuming pastime, so that we end up missing the opportunities of our own spiritual advancement.

We don't want to get drawn into *anything* to that degree. The spiritual results are too limited.

Overcome Procrastination

I have a recurring dream in which I'm back on campus. Suddenly I remember certain classes I have been forgetting to attend and will need to start soon to catch up and finish the term. Recently I had this dream again, but this time I was so far behind and the courses so difficult, I wondered if I could possibly make up the work. What do these dreams mean?

The campus is at a Temple of Golden Wisdom connected with the Param Akshar Temple. The instruction is always an ongoing study of the Shariyat, of course, but the significance for you in the physical world carries another meaning.

The Dream Master is saying that you have gotten caught up in procrastination. You are wrestling with its parent, *attachment,* a passion of the mind. This has kept you from the Spiritual Exercises of ECK and other spiritual pursuits.

You find it upsetting to be unprepared for these dream classes. Sit down with a paper and pen; and make a list of the material, financial, and spiritual parts of your life.

Straighten out the outer life, and your dream world will fall into place. One state reflects the other; it has to do with the waves of ECK that come and go.

Soul has actually wandered into a new region but has resisted picking up the ways and customs there.

This means you have reached a new level of unfold- ment inwardly, but the physical, mental, and emo- tional bodies have not kept pace. Set a new schedule of goals for yourself. Determine where you are today and where you want to be a year from now—then establish well-defined steps how you will get to that point.

This dream means: "Your mode of living life must be stepped up to keep pace with Soul. Set new goals and do this now!"

This will put you back in charge of your life again.

How to Avoid Unconscious Karma

Can we create karma in our dreams? If so, how? And how can we avoid it?

Yes, people can create karma in the dream state. Yet most are unaware that they do so, even as they are unaware of karma they make every day.

91

Each of us is like a power station. We generate energy all the time, energy that can either build or destroy. If we let unworthy thoughts or desires leave our power station, they pollute everything around us. That is bad karma. Our mind is like a machine, able to issue contaminants around the clock. Our thoughts even run on automatic at night, when we may unconsciously try to control others or harm them in the dream state.

The problem is a lack of spiritual self-discipline.

To avoid making karma, while either awake or asleep, sing HU. Sing it when you are angry, frightened, or alone. HU calms and restores, because it sets your thoughts upon the highest spiritual ideal: the trinity of the SUGMAD, the ECK, and the Mahanta.

Soul's Path to Mastership

I had a dream where someone whispered to me that I was the next Living ECK Master. What could this possibly mean?

I appreciate your question about the dream that concerned ECK Mastership. This sort of dream is not at all uncommon, as it is reported from time to time by other ECKists.

The spiritual meaning is that the Inner Master has opened the door for the next step to Mastership, but all the spiritual guidelines apply. The first is the Law of Silence, which is the measure by which one is tested to see whether he can keep to himself the secrets of heaven. Nor is the chela permitted to approach the Master with this type of dream because its true meaning is for Soul's own unfoldment and has nothing at all to do with imagined power and glory which so many mistake this position to include.

All the ECK initiations are given on the outer up to, and including, the Eighth Circle. Both outer and inner are necessary for the linkup with ECK and becoming truly established on any plane.

Practice the Law of Silence and the Law of Love. Many others are grappling with the disciplines that prepare Soul for personal Mastership.

When You See Your Future

In a recent dream I saw a situation which I understood to be a possibility in my future. Although I would eventually welcome it, I know that I am not ready for such a big step now. So I wonder why this would reveal itself to me at this time?

Dreams prepare us for the possibilities of our future. A young girl may dream of becoming a wife years before she's ready for such a role. Later, her ideas may swing away from her youthful dreams of marriage and new ones replace them.

But when the time comes for marriage, she is ready. She is ready to step into the role of a marriage partner with more love and confidence than she would have had as a girl. This is so because of her dreams.

Our dreams simply prepare us for many future possibilities. We can then decide which future path we want to go for.

Balancing the Blues

Around November and December, I am often filled with negative feelings. What causes this?

Your feelings are partly caused by the atmosphere that precedes the holiday season. However, nothing is insurmountable for Soul; It learns how to make everything into stepping-stones instead of stumbling blocks.

The holiday season generates a lot of negative energy as people find they are unable to buy the presents they would like. Also, the gifts they *do* buy are often beyond their means. A wave of this psychic energy sweeps the world every Christmas. It is especially noticeable in crowds, as people hurry to do their last-minute shopping.

This negative wave can color our own feelings and make us despondent for no real reason. But of course, the mind can always think of reasons to separate itself from the Light and Sound.

Some people who have raised themselves above the human consciousness are uncomfortable when exposed to extremes of worry, scurry, and turmoil during Christmas shopping. It is a lot like the swimmer who dives into ocean waters with fins, mask, and snorkel. He can stay underwater only as long as his lungs can hold the oxygen. So we sometimes run into stores and leave fast.

Having Patience

I worry a lot about my spiritual progress. Should I be reading more ECK books and contemplating more in order to get more inner experiences?

You have the love and protection of the Mahanta at all times. Not everyone sees visual images during contemplation or in dreams. Some people develop a feeling of the Master's presence and let it guide them around the usual obstacles. There are also those who get a touch of God's hand in some way and then are unable to find it ever again.

Please be patient, and let the ECK bring you what is good for you as you are ready. Having experiences with some of these manifestations of Light and Sound before one is prepared does nobody any good. There is no advantage to wading in water over your head.

Financial Balance

I am living with my brother and his wife in a very hostile situation. They make fun of my membership in ECKANKAR and criticize me for doing spiritual exercises for hours. I would like to move out and get my own apartment, but I am not making enough money right now. They say I am pouring all my money into ECKANKAR.

I appreciate your request for help. It is best to get one's physical and personal affairs in order first. Myself, I would use my income to get my physical life in order.

The Spiritual Exercises of ECK are meant to be done no more than twenty to thirty minutes a day unless there is an experience underway that must be completed. Slow down on the spiritual exercises, and don't spend more time on them than is suggested above.

Divine Spirit began working on your request the moment you dropped your letter in the mailbox. But we must also do our part to straighten out personal affairs. As we put effort into bringing harmony and balance into our life, then these efforts are enhanced by the subtle, often direct, intervention of the ECK.

Please use your money to take care of personal needs first, and in the meantime go a little more slowly with the spiritual exercises.

Balance is the most important thing to achieve right now.

95

Can You Serve ECK Too Much?

An ECKist recently remarked that I wasn't attending ECK meetings. This made me concerned about how to maintain a personal balance in my responsibilities to the local area as a Higher Initiate and my personal life as an ECKist. I want to be true to myself.

It was good to hear from you. To answer your question of whether to participate in local ECK activities if it does not seem right: Do what you feel inclined to do. The ECK takes each person through experiences when they're needed.

But to follow your inner direction may take diplomacy and understanding. Explain to the other H.I.'s, if you even feel it is necessary, that the Mahanta has you working quietly in the background. And when your inner direction changes toward outer service again, you'll be in touch with the ECK leaders to help where possible.

ECKists are at every level of life and must have the freedom to operate where they are suited to be.

Balance in Helping Others

I feel that my purpose in life has to do with helping others. But I am not clear as to how to do this or what exactly is my purpose for being here. Can you help?

Doing something to help others must be a personal decision. The path of ECK is one of harmony and balance. Personal duties and responsibilities are attended to first before we leave home, in a sense, to serve others.

The Spiritual Exercises of ECK are helpful initially to open ourselves to a greater flow from Divine Spirit. Yet with receiving more of Its Sound and Light

96

comes the need to give of ourselves in some manner to others. This giving, or outflow, serves to balance us in our daily life. It is best to go slow when stepping on the path of ECK, whether we wish to serve or to study.

Much of the insight you asked for will come through the Inner Master. This will come either directly or simply through a knowingness of what to do the next day upon awakening.

Trust this guidance as long as you see it to be positive. But take your time and go slowly.

The clues to your purpose in life can be found in *The Spiritual Notebook* or *The Shariyat-Ki-Sugmad*. It is better to find these answers for ourselves rather than have someone tell us.

Lessons That Teach Balance

About two years ago you appeared in a dream to me. It was a humorous setting; I think you were playing cards. Not until recently did you come again, this time with a countenance of rejection or anger at me. I tried to inspire a smile from you but to no avail. A few weeks ago you appeared in a dream with your back to me. I haven't been able to decode the message. Can you help me?

You wrote of your concern that the Inner Master rejected you three times on the inner planes. Naturally this would seem to be a grave crisis in your spiritual affairs, but this is not so if seen in the light of the lesson that the Mahanta was trying to teach you.

First of all, the Mahanta is always with you for It is the ECK. The ECK is love and encompasses all life.

But life in these worlds has a mixture of good and bad things that happen to us. It's easy to follow the

Master in the good times, but will the chela's love remain when the Master seems to turn his face away?

The test you met in the dream state, where the Mahanta seemed to reject you, is one of the many tests that a chela can use to gauge his love for the ECK. Will you love the ECK and the SUGMAD in the bad times too? There is no desolation so complete as when the chela leaves the Sound and Light. The void in his life will show up sooner or later.

This test will come in a number of different ways, but the lesson it teaches is this: How great is your love for the Mahanta? Will you love him even when he seems to have turned his back on you? A heart full of trust and love in contemplation will tell you that the Mahanta's love is returned to you a thousandfold.

Please know that I am always with you.

Do You Belong on This Path?

I've been an ECKist for about seven years. At first I was so happy, but now I feel miserable. I always read about other people's wonderful experiences, but the Sound I hear never changes in pitch and the Light is always the same color. Do you think I belong on this path?

It was good to hear from you. You're doing very well on the spiritual end of things: You see the Light and hear the Sound. Many ECKists, believe it or not, would trade places with you in an instant.

The next thing to begin on is bringing your physical life up to what you've reached spiritually.

Unless you harmonize your outer and inner sides, you will remain unhappy. A suggestion is to look more into ways of improving your outlook by a more careful diet. Also, open yourself to ECK to make you more successful in your daily pursuits. If I can be of more help, please write.

The Way to See Truth

The path to God seems so slow at times. Why does it take so long for people like me to recognize truth?

Most people have a deep longing to hear truth, but it is doubtful that many of them would know it if it were to fall on the ground in front of them. Nevertheless, the search for it is on.

Life throws problems at us: Is this the Master? Would the true teachings be done in this or that manner? The centuries turn as on a slow axle.

The wayward make their hesitant way back to the source of life when all the petty parts of them have been dissolved through the disappointments and sorrows of living. Then, and only then, is there enough consciousness embedded in the Soul body to see truth when it steps quietly before It.

Is there any meaning on earth except that the people on it must bump heads and make peace not with others, but with themselves?

Making Peace with Yourself

I am having some difficulty embracing the local community of ECKists. Ever since I became a Fifth Initiate all I've wanted to do is get some breathing space from the group consciousness. Isn't my primary goal to establish myself on this new plane?

Soul in a passive mode is off by Itself. When It is active, It is joined with other Souls in a mutual interaction. Drops in an ocean are always moving and are

99

always part of the ecology in the water system in that place. Soul is not separated from the Force of Life except by choice.

To exist means to interact in some kind of a community. This is true whether one's participation is only in the outer world, the inner world, or both the outer and inner worlds in the correct way at that time.

Someone who lives mostly in the outer consciousness is out of balance. This is the social consciousness. Someone who thrives mostly in the inner consciousness is also out of balance, but in the opposite direction. This is the isolated saint.

The balance of outer and inner spirituality is the spiritual goal in ECKANKAR. Neither too much nor too little at any particular time. That is a determination made by each person. Neither I nor anyone else can dictate what that balance is at the moment.

Too many ECK initiates in the past have tried to hide from life. They take to austerities and harsh interpretations of what truth is. They lack love and grace, two spiritual attributes. Truth considers love and grace and kindness and understanding. Someone who thinks he's living and speaking "truth" and is blunt, pigheaded, or unkind is living in the solitary prison of the mind and its passions.

If you spiritually need quiet now, just ignore invitations to outer ECK functions. Or, if the program doesn't suit you, just turn off the radio.

How Do You Stay in Balance?

Balance is often referred to as an important aspect in life. How does one get in balance—and stay there?

The ECK usually takes care of that by giving certain experiences that restore one's ability to hear spiritually.

100

Every so often an ECK initiate says to me, "Please tell me if I ever get out of balance."

Yet when that time comes, he cannot hear my guidance. He may try to follow it, but he is like a robot in his actions. So he continues to make more spiritual blunders. He simply does not understand why everything continues to go wrong even though he is following what he thinks the Master is saying.

How do you get in balance—and stay there?

Always love the SUGMAD, the ECK, and the Mahanta—no matter what happens in your outer life. Once you realize the spiritual lesson behind your imbalance, you will return naturally to the mainstream of the Audible Life Current.

In my life, how can I apply the ECK principles to the Year of Graceful Living?

The point of this theme—A Year of Graceful Living—for the spiritual year 1992–93 and beyond is to realize that everything that comes into your life is for the good. No matter how bad it may appear. The graceful part is your realization of the ECK love current that exists beyond the outer turmoil of life.

As the Outer Master, I am interested only in show-ing you the way to the temple inside yourself. This is the home of the Mahanta; many find the doorway at the heart center.

7

Questions about ECK

Is ECKANKAR really the direct path back to God?

Divine Spirit has provided many paths for Soul to take back to God. Each path roughly fits the consciousness of a like-minded group. That is why there is no reason to look down on any religious teaching. The ECK Masters come to enliven, not destroy, religious teachings, because periodically the spiritual light dims.

No one path is true for everyone. That includes Catholicism, Protestant synods, the Oriental beliefs. Many of the different Christian groups are still grappling with the Golden Rule given twenty centuries ago.

A lot of attention is put upon sects today, but the spilling of blood that was the baptism for the rise of Christian power is ignored. The karmic debts incurred by the priestcraft during the past centuries is not where one wants to put his attention. I am not criticizing Christian history, because I played my role helping in the establishment of several paths.

By now you have developed your own ways of testing whether someone's claim has any degree of truth.

Use that method and measure the teachings of ECK.

Is a path true? What are you looking for in it? In ECK, you ought to be able to see the Light and hear the Sound of God. No path on earth can promise its followers prosperity and unblemished health. That is being ignorant of facts, of how things are. A spiritual path ought to show the way to God. If you find one that does this, then follow it. If not, you must find another that fits you.

What's the Purpose of ECK?

I need to know where I am on the spiritual ladder. As the Master for the chelas in ECK, do you know me spiritually?

The purpose of the Living ECK Master is to assist one in his own efforts toward reaching God Consciousness. The path of ECK is to let one develop spiritual stamina and become a Master in his own right.

As the Outer Master, I am interested only in showing you the way to the temple inside yourself. This is the home of the Mahanta; many find the doorway at the heart center.

Put full attention on the daily affairs in your life, for this is also part of that which touches the spiritual consciousness. Go at your own pace. There is never any hurry about Soul's unfoldment to God.

Can ECK Help You?

Is ECKANKAR a secret society? How will ECK affect my life span on earth? And as the Living ECK Master, can you help me discover my best talent and conquer physical and mental problems?

I appreciate your questions. ECKANKAR is not a secret society; it is open to anyone wishing to practice the Spiritual Exercises of ECK. They are designed to expand one's consciousness at a pace that is comfortable. What one learns within himself, a conversation between himself and the Inner Master, is private and only for one's own benefit.

Generally speaking, the Spiritual Exercises of ECK slow one's body vibrations into a greater harmony. This alone would tend to increase one's health and longevity. As one's unfoldment begins, mental and emotional blocks are slowly removed so as to bring greater stability and well-being to the individual. One must make his own career decisions, however. That must be what one most wants to do and is willing to achieve through careful study and planning.

Will Your Life Change?

Should I join ECKANKAR? How will it affect my life?

Soul is listening but is timid to take the first step. And when It does, somebody must be there to give constant encouragement.

One always wonders how ready people are to hear the Word of ECK. They want to know what ECK has for them to live better lives: less fear, more love, or whatever basic needs people have.

ECK does bring change. ECKists who have been in ECKANKAR ten or fifteen years see in themselves a whole new outlook on life as it was and is. Not many ECKists would want to go back to things the way they were before ECK.

Some Higher Initiates can easily forget the blackness of life before ECK. For most of them, it was a

105

period of quiet desperation. When they found the Living ECK Master, there was an immediate recognition of the age-old friendship that was the only possible way to freedom and happiness.

How Will You Feel?

I wonder if I belong in any religion. I expect too much from religion and not enough from myself. I never felt that I was worth very much; I wanted someone else to take care of me. But ECKANKAR is asking me to take control of my spiritual and physical life.

When you spoke of wanting someone else to take care of you, it let me remember my feelings when I first came to ECK.

More than anything, I just wanted to be an average person who got his religion in church on Sunday during a one-hour service. But ECK wouldn't have it that way. As my certainty about ECK grew, I nevertheless asked many times, "God, why me?" Never with a physical answer that I could understand, the ECK was making my world wider each month.

I'm finally comfortable with ECK. More than anything, the ECK changes brought me love—the sweetest and most painful change of all.

Will ECK Make a Difference in Your Life?

How does ECKANKAR compare to other religions and teachings? At first glance, the practices seem similar.

The outer practices of ECK do look a lot like those of other groups, but most ECK initiates know there is a difference.

For example, Christian groups are meditating when

they silently sing a word, as a noise blocker (white noise). To someone who doesn't know any better, the Christian who chants a word like that and an ECKist who sings his charged word are doing exactly the same thing. And they are, if the ECKist isn't able to reach experiences in the Sound and Light of God.

It's humbling to think that despite the great size of the Catholic church, its immediate effect is actually quite small. When the ages have passed away, the only thing that will matter is how much a particular Catholic got from that particular lifetime that lasted the short breath of fifty to sixty years.

A church can be the greatest on earth, but all that matters when it comes time for someone to leave this life is whether it's made him a spiritually better person. This cuts through the grand fanfare of all religions. How much has that religion helped a particular follower in his brief lifetime? Nothing else really matters.

Hungry for Truth

Why is it that people who just join ECKANKAR sometimes seem to understand it better than those who have been in it a long time?

Sometimes that is true. Remember, though, the Mahanta works with people a long time before he lets them come into ECKANKAR. It depends upon their spiritual needs.

Have you ever played a game for the first time and surprised yourself and everyone else by how well you did? Later, when you played again, you did only so-so? Then, if you spent a lot of time in practice, you eventually got as good as that first lucky time? It can be something like that in ECK too.

107

In other cases, when new people first join ECKANKAR they are hungry for truth. Later, they may begin to take these wonderful teachings for granted and care less about them. Deep gratitude is thus a second reason why newcomers may seem to understand ECK better than some longtime members.

The general level of spiritual consciousness of people who come to ECK today is higher than that of those who came to ECK in the sixties. At the same time, those who came into ECK in the 1960s have since continued up the spiral to God. This is just a way of addressing the expanding worlds in ECK.

What Is a Co-worker with God?

A lot of changes came into my life when I found ECK. Is it all right to go slowly with my study of the teachings?

It is good that you are going slowly with the ECK works. One does find it truly difficult to make his own way in life when family and friends are going in another direction. By all means, go easy with your study of the inward things.

After you see the Light and hear the Sound, then comes the biggest challenge of all. How are you going to make the best use of this life? How are you going to build toward an experience that is rich for Soul?

The answer is reflected in the only true mission of Soul: to become a citizen of the spiritual worlds while still in the physical worlds. This is the meaning of Co-worker with God. We choose our own mission. Thus our life is always in harmony because we make it such.

A real discipline is for one to take a good look at himself, see where he is, and accept himself as a unique individual. That erases guilt and fear.

The Call of Soul

At age fifty-five, I am ready to serve God. But I wonder, Is ECKANKAR for me? Where can I find additional knowledge on this?

When Soul first hears the thin, biting call of God, it is a lonely sound. But as Soul draws closer to God in spirituality, there is supposed to be a greater sense of direction while meeting daily events.

Each person must walk his own path. No one else can do it for him. The ECK Masters can help, however, when asked to do so. They will hardly ever interfere in anyone's state of consciousness without that person's express permission. To do so is a violation of the spiritual law.

You want to know how to learn more about divine knowledge? The teachings of ECK are actually located within the heart.

The key then to the esoteric teachings lies in the Spiritual Exercises of ECK. These are simple techniques that take only minutes a day. They uplift Soul in Its state of consciousness and lead to the Light and Sound of God.

A Question of Balance

What must I give up for spiritual freedom?

The only thing we give up to Divine Spirit is the inner direction of our spiritual affairs. This does not mean giving up family, friends, or earthly possessions. The Living ECK Master does not ask this of anyone.

The purpose of the path of ECK is simply to outline the most direct route back to the heart of God. The traps and pitfalls are outlined in the writings of ECK. Learning the invisible laws that affect our every act, whether or not we are conscious of them, will allow us to straighten out our life. We find that every aspect of our personal life begins to be smoother. This follows the principle: as above, so below.

Not everyone is willing to exercise the self-disciplines that are needed to overcome the downward pull of mind and matter and ascend toward the true regions of light. This should be their choice.

There are countless states of consciousness among the children of God on this planet. The Divine Essence has provided numerous religions to fit the needs of most of these Souls. Thus we recognize other religions as offshoots of ECK, Divine Spirit. ECKANKAR is not the only path to God, but it is the most direct.

The law of the universes is that one must pay in the true coin for everything received. The Light and Sound of God are generally reached by faithful practice of the Spiritual Exercises of ECK. Changes must often be made slowly in order to maintain a balance in everyday life.

The path of ECK is not for ascetics, but for those willing to walk the middle path of total responsibility toward God-Realization.

Experiences in the Light and Sound

I'm having real spiritual problems: I want to have real communion with God. All I've seen for two years is the Blue Light; and I hear the same sound of tinkling bells, with little change in tone.

Do you know that hearing the Sound and seeing the Light is actually communion with God?

We are led to believe that communion with God is hearing a big voice in the sky. But oftentimes it comes

110

as a still small voice, not the roar from the mountaintop. The ECK may speak in a gentle way, with a nudge of how to do something, such as which lawyer or dentist to see—help that's right down to earth.

Can You Follow Two Paths?

I am considering joining ECKANKAR but am presently in another spiritual development group. Can I continue with this group and also become an ECKist?

For the present, why not finish up your study with the other spiritual development group? I couldn't recommend mixing the ECK teachings with the other group. It causes a lot of confusion and overloads our capacity to make any headway in a single direction.

Following two paths at a time usually causes unnecessary trouble, because we are actually splitting up the energies within us. It is the same principle as No man can have two Masters.

Take time with your other studies. There is never any hurry in following the spiritual teachings of ECK.

Make Your Own Decisions

When I came upon an ECK book, I tried some of the contemplative exercises. The sounds I heard were very familiar to me. As a child of five, I used to hear them. In this ECK book, I discovered many answers to things I have asked for years. But I am not sure if I should rush into this teaching. What do you think?

I am happy you found answers to some lifelong questions. That is a good way to start an investigation of another path.

Continue with your life as you have been doing. There is no need to hurry into anything until you have examined several of the ECK books. Really consider if this teaching fits you. It is usually better if one makes all the decisions for himself, without any influence by another person.

Your background has made it possible for you to have contact with the Light and Sound, the twin aspects of Divine Spirit. If you find things going too fast in the coming days, put aside the ECK books and do other things you like. My only concern is to link up the Soul that is ready with the Audible Life Current, Divine Spirit.

Proof You Are Soul

What is Soul?

Opinions about Soul outnumber people's opinions about politics. People who *know*—actually know, not just believe—that Soul outlives death enjoy happy, creative lives. The rest are miserable and afraid.

People who fear hell fall for the trap that Soul can be burned by fire. That's really sad. Soul exists because God loves It. Its destiny is to become a Co-worker with God.

Plato told of the separation of Soul from the body. The old Greek mystery schools taught their students that Soul could reach the altar of God through certain secret methods. The students spent a few minutes a day with unique contemplative exercises that opened them little by little to the Light and Sound of God. That gave them unshakable proof that Soul lives forever.

Who do you know who has made a real study of the Light and Sound of God? It is known that the Light may be blue or white, and the Sound like a rushing wind, the music of woodwinds, or the single note of a flute.

Did Moses find the Light and Sound of God in the burning bush? Surely the Apostles did experience the Holy Spirit at Pentecost. What about Saul's conversion on the road to Damascus? ECKANKAR is a way that somebody such as you or I can bend the odds a little in favor of our having such experiences.

For Those Who Want God

Who will ECKANKAR be attracting in the coming years?

Those who really want to find God will come to ECKANKAR in the next few years. A Higher Initiate in Tennessee said, "Individuals who have been only slightly aware of ECK are now stepping to the front and sincerely asking, 'How can I find God?'"

Those who are Arahatas in the coming years will meet these people and have special opportunities of unfoldment through their service of teaching. Teaching is the best way to learn. You will find many spiritual rewards come from being a channel for the ECK.

Which Path Is the Right One?

I am at the crossroads. Is ECK the right path for me at this time?

Only you can answer that. God has put a path here to fit everyone.

In the lands of Spirit, unlike earth, there is no separation to distinguish one path from another. But earth is a training ground where Soul faces hard choices to pick what suits It now. Tomorrow It may embrace some other teaching because of a change in outlook.

Survival takes some sort of order. The orderly arrangement of planets in our solar system shows this. Without order the planets would leave their orbits and destroy each other. Same for Soul, because It's got to find Its niche in the scheme of things.

Which path fits you best? You must answer your own question. Honestly though, what more can come of your search than a hope to find God?

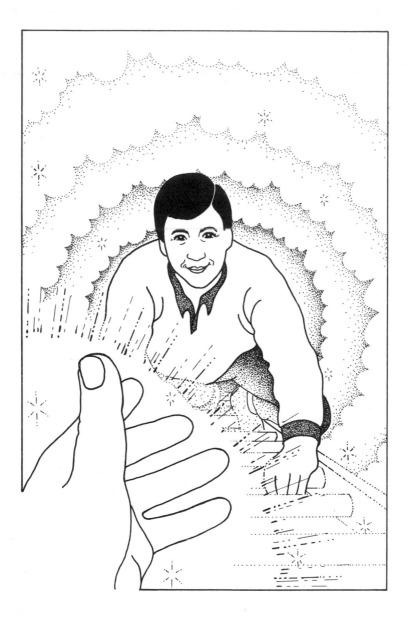

There comes a time when we realize that our efforts at unfoldment are only personal. Besides the Inner Master, no one can help us up the ladder to God.

8

Change and Growth

What is the ultimate goal of Soul?

Here is a brief review of the final goal of Soul: It gathers an education in the lower worlds so that It can become a true citizen in the spiritual community. This is what we call a Co-worker with God.

The relationship between parent and child in the worlds of matter is based on this spiritual design. The parent is the vehicle for the child's entrance into the world and is responsible for his education. The child must, between birth and the age of perhaps eighteen, learn all the dos and don'ts of his culture. The significant fact underlying the parent-child relationship is that there is more freedom for the child as he gets older and assumes more responsibility. The parent has failed his duties if the child reaches legal age and is unfit to take his place in the world.

The path of ECK encourages the freedom and responsibility of Soul. After all, that is Its birthright.

Every Soul is a spark of God. The child learns by making errors, but the wise parent must let the child learn for himself, giving guidance when it is necessary.

117

Spiritual Progress

If I don't get a reply when I write to you, I wonder if I'm doing all right. How's my spiritual progress?

I regret that not every person who writes gets a personal reply, but the demands upon my time are many.

The Living ECK Master wants to link up Soul with the Mahanta, the Inner Master. This connection is everlasting and unbreakable unless the individual breaks the tie himself. The inner connection is the whole point of the ECK teachings.

Be not so concerned about your spiritual progress. There comes a time when we realize that our efforts at unfoldment are only personal. Besides the Inner Master, no one can help us up the ladder to God. Yet we enjoy our family and companions, for together we learn the ways of ECK.

Cave of Purification

What exactly is the cave of purification?

This is an actual location on a number of planes. Its purpose is to provide a place for a rapid burn-off of karma. The cave on the Astral Plane is in a mountainous area.

The mouth of the cave is tall enough to allow for twice the height of an average-size man. There is a huge boulder to the right of the entrance as you face the cave. A smaller rock, waist high, is on the left as you approach.

Some, but not all, Second Initiates are brought here in the dream state. The Mahanta leads them into the cave where a brilliant white light burns away useless karmic burdens. The fire is white, but the flames throw no heat in the usual way. It is a fire that burns the atoms in one clean.

Sometime after this rite of purification, the individual is cleared to pass into the Causal Plane.

Are You Still Growing?

It is my nature to wish to know the next step before the present one is taken. Lately, I am not being given that luxury. The wind of change screams in my being, "This time you must take your ship out of sight of shore." Do you have any tips to help me know if I'm on the right track spiritually?

Life does throw us into circumstances that are always a bit of a challenge. And nothing is so dark as when the ECK urges us to step into the great unknown.

From experience, I find that I'm always on the frontier of my own abilities. This proves that there is always an avenue we haven't trod: one more step to the heavenly kingdom that is in us.

Follow the ECK; see where It leads you. There is never any separation from It except in consciousness, so the worlds are at your feet. All that counts is what you do in them.

I appreciate your continued efforts to bring the message of ECK, the Light and Sound, to all who are ready for It. We're all going through growing pains. And painful as the experience is, I still much prefer the pain of unfoldment to that of stagnation.

What about Physical Limitations?

I have been partially paralyzed for much of my adult life. I read in one of the ECK books that no man

*with a defective body can ever become a spiritual trav-
eler. This has really confused me, since I always felt
that I would overcome this.*

I got your question about whether certain people
can qualify as candidates for spiritual travelers despite physical conditions.

Soul is not bound by any physical limitations. The
works of ECK bring out the eternal truths from a
number of different approaches. One can choose that
which fits him.

Some people are turned aside by what they consider to be incorrect grammar used by the ECK Masters,
not realizing that the true spiritual foundation is set
in the Light and Sound of God. At times the understanding of the human consciousness is not able to
mentally comprehend the Master's words. All that's
left then is to trust in the heart, and take our questions to the inner temple.

There is no spiritual limitation unless we ourselves
allow it. Does this answer your question?

Surrender

*What's the easiest way to bring about changes in
one's life? I have been struggling for some time to improve
my outer life but can't seem to figure out how to do it.*

When one gives up and lets go of his opinions about
a situation, then Divine Spirit, the ECK, will open the
door to a new spiritual vista. You will find that when
you allow changes to occur on the inner planes, there
are also changes in the outer life.

Each step in the higher worlds must be earned in
some manner. Ultimately, however, it is simply a matter
of surrender to the Inner Master, which is the ECK.

120

Evolution of Ideas

I'm a newcomer to ECK and have some difficulty with the books I have read by Paul Twitchell. I'm not a feminist, but his ideas on women seem quaint. Can you explain how his work fits into the current path of ECK?

The Living ECK Master writes and speaks for the consciousness of his times. It's natural to find some of Paul's ideas of twenty years ago quaint today. Times change, and so does the ability of people to perceive truth better.

Your views about ECK and life in general will undergo many changes. In a few years, you will look back and hardly recognize yourself as the person you are today.

Do You Feel Unworthy?

I just got my Fifth Initiation. I had given up hope in that direction and had made up my mind to live the best I could just being an ECKist. I drive for public transit in a big city, and after long periods behind the wheel I find it very hard to be nice. Then I get down on myself for not being a good representative of ECK.

Thank you for sticking by me all these centuries and years. I still feel unworthy of this honor. I don't know what to do to help you, and I dearly wish to.

Welcome to the Fifth Circle of Initiation in ECK. You surrendered the little self and made it possible to enter into the Soul Plane permanently. Don't worry, an initiate may be uncomfortably aware of his lack of perfection, but nothing is ever perfect anyway.

The ECK is lifting you into the higher areas of God, indirectly but surely. All outer changes are a result of

121

whatever spiritual progress has been made till now. And more will come, of course. That is the nature of unfoldment.

All who love the SUGMAD stand in humility before IT and their fellow beings. Outwardly, we endeavor to let the Light of ECK shine through us to those still searching for truth. Not by sermons, but by the love and compassion in us for the gift of the Mahanta's love to us.

Fear of Change

Although I have a great love for you and the works of ECK, there have always been times of uncertainty and fear of change. Sometimes I fear that, even with all my hope, love, and dedication, I might fall. I do not want to fail myself or God. Where is the assurance that we can be guided back if we go astray?

Your concerns about failing to reach God-Realization are well taken. Life is uncertain, especially when we use outer signs to judge our inner state of consciousness.

There never can be failure in our quest for the Divine Awareness if we absolutely fix our complete attention upon the Sound and Light. The trouble comes when we slip off our spiritual center and become concerned with outer relationships—and then let this concern reflect back into our inner worlds and distort our spiritual reality.

No matter what outer events arise to throw us off our spiritual center, we must return to the Sound and Light. We must lock onto them as the only things certain of our trust.

The Mahanta is the manifested Sound and Light. Life is acknowledged to be a stormy sea. Yet so often when the boat rocks we fly into a panic, as if a boat shouldn't rock in a storm.

The storms of life separate the cosmic sailors from the meek landlubbers. It is the Way of ECK. Look always to the Light and Sound of God within you, and you will always sail the cosmic sea of ECK.

An Instrument of Change

As an ECK leader I had to discuss an unpleasant situation with a chela in my area. Later I had a dream with this person, and it seemed to contradict my understanding of the situation. The light in the dream was very bright and clear, and it contrasted with my feeling that there was something wrong. Was I used by the ECK or the Kal in this situation?

Your perceptions about this situation were on track. The ECK used you as Its instrument to bring about spiritual changes. Its ways are often mysterious, but Its end will be clearly seen by all who need to know it.

Our role is to act in good faith and love. You've done that. Please rest easy about whether you interpreted things correctly in the past. You simply acted as a clear channel for the Mahanta. The best course now is to give love and keep the door open.

You have felt the weight that can come upon a leader's shoulders. Fortunately such times as you went through are the exception, rather than the rule. The experience brought you more wisdom and love. Please continue as you have—in the Light and Sound.

Cycles of Change

I feel a sort of sadness when one cycle ends in my life and another begins. Can you explain this?

123

Life teaches that all living beings go through cycles of change. This does not mark the end of your spiritual opportunities but another beginning.

Soul operates in cycles of activity and rest. The ECK sees, and indeed sets, the grand design of our lives. It gives us choices that we accept and grow from.

A good thought might be, Hold fast to ECK, but let go of those things that pass. In that light, you will never stand in your own way.

You, and all leaders in ECK, need to rest from time to time. The work creates a lot of wear and tear. Use your time now to teach those who want truth; learn from them. Living can be a joy. It should give us a sense of wonder and love.

What Mistakes Mean

I have always been afraid of making mistakes. As an ECK leader, this attitude has been especially difficult for me. But I can't seem to let it go. Can you help?

Learning means making errors. Those learning to be ECK leaders make errors just the way anyone does when he is growing.

I don't mind an error as long as the individual benefits from it, picks up the pieces, and goes on—a wiser individual.

Finding Your Personal Pace

I am very shy and have difficulty expressing myself. I want to help spread the ECK message, but speaking in public terrifies me. Is there something wrong with me? Do I have to change myself radically before I can serve the ECK?

Divine Spirit begins to straighten out the affairs of the ECKist who follows Its way. Yet It never hurries one, for in matters of the Soul consciousness one must be opened gradually.

There are many ways we can give to Spirit, and we have the freedom to do what is comfortable for us. If you are uncomfortable in meeting people publicly to serve as an ECK vehicle, do something quietly that you want to do, even if no one else knows it. The company of a Higher Initiate will certainly uplift one, if there is an opportunity to help out in a small way.

We can be vehicles for Divine Spirit merely by declaring ourselves such in the morning: "I declare myself a vehicle for the SUGMAD, the ECK, and the Mahanta." This can be done silently—even while shopping! Then just be!

Most important in the spiritual works of ECK is the knowledge that a solution to every problem is within us.

9

Creativity and Self-Discipline

I often hear ECKists describe very personal experiences. This makes me wonder, What constitutes the Law of Silence?

The Law of Silence is a spiritual principle that draws a very fine line. If you have an experience that may help another person understand his own, then tell it in a fitting way.

Also be sure that telling your experience will really help that person. Sometimes we like to brag about our imagined superior spiritual development.

You can tell when you've said too much: Your stomach will knot up; you'll feel uncomfortable. It takes some people a long time to learn to watch their own bodies as a sensitivity meter about how their words affect others. But you can learn to do it.

The Law of Silence is easier to learn if you're more willing to just listen to others instead of having to pummel them with your great wisdom.

Someone once said, "Life's too short to make all the mistakes yourself. So learn from those of others."

How can I be sure which spiritual experiences should not be discussed?

The way of ECK is one of experience. Use the trial-and-error method to see which inner experiences are too sacred for public discussion.

Keep track of your inner experiences for a given period of time and talk of them to your usual confidants. What happens is that the Mahanta begins to shut down the individual's memory of the secret teachings that are given to him. Within a month or two, you will become aware that the golden hand of the Mahanta's love and protection has been withdrawn. You will feel empty and alone.

When you are convinced of the emptiness that comes of giving the secret teachings of the Mahanta to those who have no right to them, then make it a practice to keep all the inner happenings to yourself. It will take one to two months before the channel to the ECK will open you to the secret teachings again.

This experiment can be done as often as proof is needed that the secret instructions of the Mahanta are for you alone. Finally, one's self-discipline becomes such that he tells no one but the Master anything, because the penalty of living without the love and protection of the Mahanta is not worth the trouble.

Self-Discipline and Inertia

I still cannot manifest things in my life that I desire. I have guilt feelings because I don't have any self-discipline. Before, I didn't depend on anyone but myself, but along the way, I lost this mastery of self. I recently saw an ad for a book about creative visualization. Would this help?

ECKists are such a happy lot. But what's so great about knowing that life is continuous, if it will always be a struggle with no end to having to learn new things? Please show me how to break this stalemate.

It was good to hear from you even though life has got you down. As you said, it is hard to overcome the inertia that prevents self-discipline. The ECK works are to give us ideas: how we can approach our problems in ways that bring a degree of peace and contentment.

Most important in the spiritual works of ECK is the knowledge that a solution to every problem is within us. If you find the book on creative visualization helpful, please use it to help you pull free from the immobility in which you find yourself.

The human consciousness can act like a pit of quicksand, always pulling us down relentlessly. The spiritual exercises are the linkup to Divine Spirit. They are a rope we can use to pull ourselves free from this sort of despondency.

What is our goal? Manifesting material things is not the goal of saints, although most start out trying to accomplish this as a first step. The biblical saying is true in that we seek first the Kingdom of God and all things shall be added to us.

The cycle of creative action begins with the concept we carry in our minds of what we wish to do. The next step is to outline on paper some plan of how to accomplish this. The final step is action in carrying out the plan.

This is the mysterious Rule of Threes that lies behind every successful creative venture. Another way of saying this is that a project must be seen in the light of three essential elements: the positive, the negative, and the unseen but essential neutralizing element still undiscovered by science as the catalyst.

Set your plans up in some structure of threes because that is the formula that embodies the creative principle.

Resisting Downward Pulls

I have a craving for narcotics, which are at my disposal as a nurse. I'm feeling very angry at myself and guilty. Help!

The pull of drugs and alcohol is almost more than one can shake off by himself. Consider exploring a drug-abuse program that will not jeopardize your nursing career. Divine Spirit helps us when we take the first step ourselves.

The ECK Masters have had to face every test of the initiate in their struggle for the God Consciousness. The divine promise of Soul is that every problem contains a solution. The key is self-discipline and surrender of the mental habits to the Mahanta.

What can help me break the hold of depression? I find myself very dispirited about my marriage and life in general.

There are several ways to break the negative hold that you have upon you. One is to lift yourself above this negativity through a spiritual exercise. For this I recommend the Easy Way technique found on page 11 of my book *The Living Word.*

The second part is to get counseling. Try the Family Service Association that is listed in the phone book. This is a positive step because the people there are willing to help you find the next step in your life.

The whole point about Soul incarnating in the world is so that It can master every situation that develops in Its life. This is the self-mastery that is spoken of so much in the ECK works. We arrange our lives so that we come into harmony with the laws of ECK. Whatever decision we make, it is done in the name of the Mahanta. It results in good for everyone concerned.

There is no way to bow out of life and think we've cheated our due lessons. It may sound harsh, but the troubles we have are of our own making. Furthermore, the solution to all trouble also lies within the abilities of Soul to rise above and work from the whole viewpoint. This comes through the expansion of consciousness that is attained through faithful practice of the Spiritual Exercises of ECK.

Divine Spirit often begins working for our welfare after we have made some small effort first. The love and protection of Spirit surround you at all times but must be accepted with a loving heart.

I've been unable to discipline myself in the area of drugs. I feel I am trying to pursue two paths at once, the path of ECK and the path of Kal.

You're being honest with yourself. I respect that. A spiritual path that's suitable for you will build upon your abilities and interests and lead you to God-Realization. Only you can, and should, decide what is truth for you.

A person trying to mix ECK and recreational drugs does untold damage to his own spiritual unfoldment as well as that of others. I generally ask an ECKist to step aside from the path of ECK until free of the drug habit. This is done as much out of compassion for that individual as it is a discipline. It becomes a grave spiritual violation when someone introduces another person to drugs. The Lords of Karma take that case.

Does Smoking Affect
Your Spiritual Growth?

Many years back, before I joined the path of ECK, a Rosicrucian friend told me that smoking cigarettes sends Spirit away from the smoker. Some time ago I read in the Mystic World *that when one smokes, the Mahanta steps aside and watches.*

Some ECKists speak as if smoking tobacco overcomes or does harm to the Mahanta. My question is: What does smoking cigarettes do to the Mahanta or Spirit?

Smoking does not harm the Mahanta. He much prefers air unpolluted by smoke. An ECKist who smokes tells the Master that his habit is more important to him than the things of Divine Spirit. Until the chela gives it up, the Mahanta has little to offer him in the way of spiritual gifts.

I am a truck driver and on the road most of the time. I have tried to quit smoking for many years. I have been in ECK for twenty years and have never seen the Blue Star or the Inner Master. For a long time I have felt spiritually dead. It seems I have been rewarded materially instead of spiritually. I want so much to be a knowing spiritual being, but I feel that my smoking habit is keeping me from that. Please help.

Thanks for your letter about smoking and what seems to be a lack of spiritual progress. Some habits are deeply ingrained. No one expects them to go away immediately. What seems to be a long time to us—ten to twenty years—is only the blink of an eye for Soul.

You cannot measure spirituality by the number of bad habits you have or not. Nor by a certain number of experiences. Awareness of the moment and a joy for living can also be an indication of where you are spiritually.

Some, like you, are given spiritual gifts through an abundance of material goods. Appreciate those things, because they are the gifts of the ECK.

Fasting from Bad Habits

What is a mental fast? How would you describe it?

A mental fast is simply putting one's attention on the Mahanta for a twenty-four-hour period. Another way is to take every negative thought that comes to mind and throw it into a wastebasket.

The mental fast is important. It is done on Friday, and on that day the initiate thinks and acts in a refined way around people. The fast is a discipline to put one's attention upon the Inner Master. The individual who puts it there is acting in the name of the Mahanta. This cuts down the daily karma between himself and others.

Higher Initiates are held to account for daily karma. If a driver speeds seventy-five miles per hour in a fifty-five-mile-per-hour zone and gets caught, there is a fine to pay. No matter how one tries to fool himself that he is above the Law of Karma, the fine must be paid.

The mental fast uplifts the ECK initiate's state of consciousness by changing old mental structures and ideas. Thus he treats life with more reverence and looks at it with new eyes.

Facing Yourself Honestly

I had to admit to a grave mistake I made in the local ECK community. I revealed to others some private

133

material that I should have kept to myself. It was a matter of obvious indiscretion on my part. It seems more attractive sometimes to remain in silent guilt than to tell the truth.

It took uncommon courage to face up to what you said and did. Just the other day I was giving my wife examples of times I had to own up to some uncomfortable creations of my own. Each time I wished I could die.

You were tested by the Mahanta on self-responsibility. The test was not in choosing whether or not to use material of a private nature, but of ultimately accepting the responsibility for your actions.

Self-honesty is one of the most difficult tests that one will ever encounter. I will go a thousand extra miles out of my way for someone who has made an error but admits it. Your insight, understanding, and compassion are needed now more than ever in your duties as ECK Initiator and ECK Spiritual Aide. Glad to still have you aboard.

Everyone who serves the ECK with openness and honesty always receives Its protection.

Your Spiritual Survival

I have a terrible time getting along with one of the other ECK leaders in my area. I don't want to bring this small meanness to your ears, but it is difficult to watch as this person brings others to tears with rude remarks. For my own survival, I have had to back away from local meetings where this person is in charge. Can you help me understand what is happening?

Whenever an ECK initiate runs tight control on other people, he is often allowed to run freely. The ECK gives him plenty of warnings so that he might catch himself. The Mahanta may not interrupt him in his errors because a cycle that's begun is allowed to run its course.

If the cycle is stopped short of natural completion, the offender must take up the load again farther down the path. This may be done if his actions grow in their outrageousness, because there are limits to what I will allow, even if an individual is right in the middle of learning valuable lessons. When too many people are hurt too deeply spiritually, then the Mahanta brings the offender's actions to a gradual slowing.

If you feel more comfortable working in the background for the present, please feel free to do so. You must position yourself for spiritual survival.

When to Take Action, When Not

I've been trying to work with another ECKist on a team I am responsible for. But we have a hard time getting along. I have tried to surrender this to the ECK, but I don't know if I am avoiding doing something I should do.

You know how to surrender to the ECK to handle your life. A person is obligated to do all he can for himself, but when his best efforts fail, then he turns the whole bundle over to Divine Spirit to see how it can be done the right way.

It is especially trying to run into somebody who tells you to your face that your way of doing things is wrong and that he will not abide by your wishes, when you are the party responsible for the handling of it.

That is a good time to step back and say, "If that's what you think is right, OK, we'll try it your way." That is, of course, provided his way is not totally off the wall.

135

What do I do when I hear something really awful—perhaps illegal—about someone I respect in ECK?

You'd be surprised how often people complain to me about the faults of others—often without any kind of proof, just hearsay. I would do a great disservice to all the members of ECK if I acted upon allegations.

If someone comes to me and says, "So and so caused me injury," I tell them to gather the facts in the case and present them to the civil and criminal authorities. Let the law decide the case; the court system is the proper place for the airing of criminal and civil grievances. We support the process of due justice.

To act and speak about alleged misdeeds without proof or without being a principal in the case makes one subject to charges of slander or libel. If someone is found guilty by the courts of cheating others out of their life's savings or any other illegal act, *then* I am free to put them under spiritual discipline and remove them from their leadership positions in ECK.

We must be careful not to let ourselves be victims of hearsay, but always encourage the *principals* to go to the civil authorities for the due process of law. Otherwise, we may ourselves be the perpetrators of a great wrong upon the innocent.

Answering Spiritual Questions

What's the best way to work on the inner to get answers to spiritual questions and develop a relationship with the Inner Master?

The Easy Way technique is an opportunity in learning to rely on the Inner Master. Mentally ask your question while you're doing the Easy Way technique and again ask it before dropping off to sleep at night.

The answer will come, sometimes in an obvious manner. Other times it comes subtly—through the advice of a friend, a humorous anecdote, or as a symbolic dream that you develop the knack of interpreting for yourself.

List all your questions on a sheet of paper. A month later, review them to see if any have resolved themselves. Do this with all your questions every month and send a report, if you like, regarding the results.

Initiate Reports

Please share with me the spiritual reason for initiate reports. Do you read them all?

I received your initiate report from June 1 and want to thank you for understanding the importance of sending it. Writing the report, no matter how brief, is like an expression of love. Gratitude for the good things that the ECK has already given us keeps our relationship with the Mahanta open and warm.

Trusted initiates help me with the mail. It's physically impossible to service thousands of people by myself. But I choose to see certain classes of mail. Your reports come to my desk regularly. Sometimes I want to write and say, "Yes, your letters are read." But you know that already.

When one sends an initiate report, it is an act of spiritual surrender—of attachments to old ideas, etc. As with money, so with initiate reports—lend no more than you can afford to lose. The reports are to give chelas the opportunity to unload their mental, emotional, and spiritual burdens.

It is up to each person how much he wishes to gain from my offer. No one is forced to write an initiate report.

There are many letters that come across my desk—letters from the happy, the ill, the young, the broken-hearted. As the Inner Master I can be with each individual in the hour of greatest joy or need.

You may hold inner conversations with me, if you like, because in Soul body I am always with you. A deep love for life is what carries one eventually into the Ocean of Love and Mercy. Love attracts love, and all the spiritual blessings of the SUGMAD are given unto you.

Action as Self-Discipline

What kind of self-discipline is needed to get through a particularly difficult time—such as the death of someone close?

Although one's mind pretends to understand the parting at translation, the heart does not. Keep yourself active in the weeks ahead, for that will dim the loneliness.

Privilege of Life

My husband killed himself. I feel great pain and loneliness, and so do my children. Can you help me understand why my husband did this and what I can do to heal? Why do people commit suicide?

Life simply becomes too much of a burden for some because they look for spiritual love but can't find it. They feel they have no choice but to end the impasse by taking their own life.

Your husband is in a class now so he can get a fuller understanding of the privilege of coming into a physical body for spiritual maturity. He did not understand this. This does not mean he's put in some kind of hell

138

for a certain time, because the spiritual structure is designed to educate, rather than punish, those people who harm themselves by suicide.

The greatest misunderstanding is thinking that a spiritual giant has to withdraw from life in order to be successful with the God Consciousness. Nothing could be further from the truth.

One can always take his life, of course. This does not lead to God, but it leads back to a baby body almost immediately. Then all the tests and trials start over again until Soul comes to know what it means to become a Co-worker with God. When people write me about this, I usually tell them to seek a trained, licensed counselor who can help them understand some of the responsibilities that go along with living.

All too often a person has damaged himself emotionally and mentally through austerities before he found the path of ECK, the spiritual way that teaches balance and moderation in all departments of living. By then, their only real aid must come through licensed medical and counseling practitioners.

Self-destruction is not the way. How can one leave the worlds of ECK?

The Purpose of Music

Do certain types of music affect people negatively? If so, how?

Let's say this: The music you like tells a lot about you. Some music is uplifting, while other music is not. Certain music is harsh, yet that does not mean it is not music. Take, for example, the music of the Chinese, Japanese, and Indian people. It may hurt the ears of many people in the West, as does bagpipe music. Yet it is the choice of millions. So what is negative music?

Usually, it is music not to our liking.

Music can break up thought forms in a society. For example, look at the music of Elvis Presley and the Beatles. At first, the media made fun of it. That soon changed.

Teens' music is sure to offend parents, and vice versa. Music, like anything else, becomes very negative when we try to push our tastes off on others—like blaring our music in public. An ECKist has a high regard for the rights of others.

And yes, many people do serious harm to their ears by playing music too loudly through headsets. That is a very negative side of music—though of volume and not of kind.

Write Down Your Experiences

Tell me the purpose of writing down spiritual experiences. I would like to work on a book of my own. Is there any benefit to ECKANKAR or the world in general?

You may miss the connection at first between the mission of the Living ECK Master and the life of Portugal's Henry the Navigator, of the early fifteenth century. Henry actually set up the conditions that enabled Columbus to discover America.

Until Henry's day, sea charts were closely guarded secrets. Many of them reflected errors of the clergy, whose maps tried to rest upon their understanding of the Bible. Henry changed all that.

Portugal became a country committed to exploration. Henry required the sailors to debrief after each voyage. Every bit of new travel information was incorporated into maps that marked latitude and longitude. Slowly, Portuguese sailors pushed back the walls of ignorance that enclosed the world then.

That's what the Living ECK Master is doing today: The sailors of the Cosmic Sea are recording their journeys into the unknown world beyond the physical plane.

This is the purpose of their spiritual journals, their initiate reports, and the books and articles they write. We must compile this information in the interest of spiritual survival. Many hands will contribute to this mission as best they can.

Do you see the point?

Writing has opened up a whole new world for me. Is it possible to heal the past through what we write?

A writer's work can be a revelation to the writer. As you transcend the daily reality, it's found to be a mask that covers old feelings, old fears.

The process of writing uncovers our own deepest thoughts and emotions, then transforms them into a medium of teaching for others. We can change the future through an understanding and reconciliation of the past.

Creative Success

What does it take to become really successful at a creative pursuit like writing, music, or art?

It really makes very little difference what we choose to do with our talents and interests. Life in ECK just means that we live life to the hilt.

Writing is a very difficult undertaking. If your interest is in writing, you must immerse yourself in it. That means writing and reading a lot. Read to learn, and write to give.

Study your audience. For whom are you writing? Let's say you did a humor piece for *Reader's Digest*. What are their needs? Once you understand their needs, you can either meet them or look for another outlet that fits your style. You may have the greatest article in the world, but it's got to get past the editor before anyone in the world will read it. So, please the editor. Learn about his needs in *Writer's Market* and *Writer's Digest*.

Whatever you plan to do, find something you really want to do—and are willing to sweat and labor for without recognition. The Mahanta sometimes teaches surrender in the most down-to-earth ways.

Why ECK Writers?

What's the purpose of having ECK writers?

My goal is to preserve the individuality of one. Soul is a unique creation. When man-made laws try to abridge the individual freedoms, then I and the ECK writers give information from the ECK viewpoint so people can make a choice for themselves.

Gear your writing to the public, with a slight bridge to the ECK teachings in a gentle way, if you can.

Creative Channels

What roles do discipline and imagination play in being a creative vehicle for ECK? I would like to be a writer someday.

The little book, *Harold and the Purple Crayon*, illustrates the creative principle of the imagination.

All success begins with the imagination that pulls together the ethereal substance. Then discipline takes the next step and plans how to bring the concept or invention down into the physical reality. This little book is a wonderful example of Soul working through Its imagination.

For those of us who labor over a typewriter or computer, this form of creative expression ranges from agony to ecstasy. When the ethereal idea reaches the paper in a clean, easy-to-understand way, then there is the satisfaction of having successfully made a bridge between heaven and earth.

Remember how the grade-school teacher used to make you diagram English sentences? It is a surprise to see what turns up when the same technique is used on published writers in a successful magazine. Does the writer begin with several short, catchy examples that illustrate the principle that he is about to present to you, the reader? Is the whole thing done through the story form? How is a problem given, and in what manner does the writer draw a solution?

My observation has shown that if I want to learn to do a thing well, the idea is to find somebody who is an expert in the field of my interest. This applies especially to writing.

Universities offer writing classes. This is a good way to get the discipline to start putting words on paper. It is nothing more, after all, than learning how to sit down and arrange thoughts into a step-by-step pattern that is familiar and enjoyable to the reader.

The best rule of thumb to finding a writer to use as an ideal is first of all: Does he sell? Secondly, ask yourself, Do I like his stories?

The writing style must, above all, be a simple one. Simple and alive! Let your writing have time to "cure" between rewrites. Good writing is done through re-writing.

I am an ECK musician and would like to know the best kind of music to compose to spread Divine Spirit's message. What spiritual purpose does ECK music have?

Have you noticed what a challenge it is to present the ECK message? Something always tends to come up so that one feels it's easier to quit than go ahead with the performance. But in life as on stage, a trooper keeps on going. ECK music opens the heart of Soul.

As to what kind of music to compose in ECK: Simply, people have to like it. A song touches many because of the beautiful melody. The dictionary says a melody is "a sweet or agreeable succession or arrangement of sounds." Depending upon the skill of the composer, that touches people.

Music has to break loose and soar somewhere in its presentation, with melody.

In writing, Shakespeare's works are for the highbrow today. But when he wrote them, they were popular works for the masses (like Steven Spielberg and his movies). The hot blood of life once coursed through Shakespearean plays, but the language is outmoded now. Few can understand it.

Music must be alive today if it expects to be a classic years from now. As a composer, you probably have several ideas of how to approach this challenge.

So few know what a love for living means. They've put a web around themselves and called it ECK. Life is a celebration. Some will read that as wanton living, but true celebration is loving God and ITS own.

You hear the Music. Follow It; don't lose It. Listen to the Mahanta and write what you will.

144

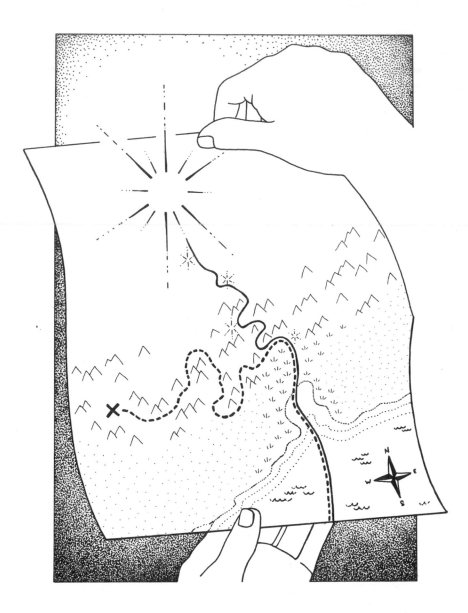

Therefore, if the ECK brings a new direction into our life, which falls outside our original master plan, we contemplate upon it. We are willing to change our direction.

10

Spiritual Goals

A friend of mine told me he had gotten God-Realization by chanting the word from the Ninth Plane. So I started doing it too, setting a date of three months for God-Realization. What else should I do?

I found the story of your friend's God-Realization experience of interest.

A word of caution: Check the motives of somebody who says he has a state of consciousness from the highest plane, especially when you are without a yardstick to measure it. See if his claims are not to get influence over you.

The God-illumined beings are humble; they don't need recognition to be Co-workers with God. They are generally happy people, not given over to moods; for what greater pleasure is there than service to the SUGMAD?

Impostors run up and down the emotional band. The unimaginable power of ECK is supposedly a force that drives them without mercy, thereby accounting for their erratic behavior swings.

It is all right to set a date for God-Realization as

Paul Twitchell did. When it comes, however, you will be the most surprised of anyone, for it comes on silent feet.

Spiritual Purpose

How do I know my purpose in this lifetime?

You know your *general* purpose is to become a Co-worker with God. So how do you identify your *personal* goal?

Let's say you're a writer planning to write a novel. It is the story of your life. You may drive your story by one of two approaches: by plot or character. Let me explain.

If you plan your life by plot (a master plan), the rest of your life will reflect your spiritual unfoldment at the time of planning. This is a narrow approach. You will reject any experience outside the original plan. It leaves no room for freedom.

A plot-driven story has every detail planned. However, it creates a character (you) whose understanding of life is thin, like a piece of cardboard. Such a person is stiff, afraid of people's opinions. Failure crushes him easily. He or she weighs every act according to an outside authority, such as what people might think.

On the other hand, a character-driven story is like a life guided by the Sound and Light of God. Yes, we do plan. However, in this approach, we recognize the superiority of Soul over any plan. Therefore, if the ECK brings a new direction into our life, which falls outside our original master plan, we contemplate upon it. We are willing to change our direction.

This character-driven approach to living is fresh. It can accept spontaneity. We see the ECK's guidance as a moment-to-moment reality. It is a better guide than our mind, which creates the plot-driven life.

So how do you learn your purpose?

The Mahanta will bring you many right seasons for spiritual growth. Contemplate upon them. Only at the end of your life will you be certain of what your personal goal was, and if you have achieved it.

In the meantime, plan for a full, rich life of love and service to God and others.

Let's say that a chela has a dream, goal, or service in mind. How does it fit with his unfoldment to God-Realization?

If an act or plan is selfless, it will aid a chela's spiritual quest.

The ECK, or Holy Spirit, can lift the most common beginning to the highest good. Yet, to succeed, we must first surrender our little self to achieve divine love. How can we do that?

An unselfish dream, goal, or service can help us to the height of spiritual living. To reach it, we must develop a complete love for God. So, we first make an inner agreement to love the SUGMAD, and then life itself will supply what we need to achieve divine love.

Eventually, every dream, goal, or service meets in the Experience of God, which makes us over into a new spiritual being.

Are You a Co-worker with God?

In an ECK Worship Service a couple of weeks ago, someone brought up a good question which I would like to ask you. If the goal of every chela is to become a Co-worker with God, what are we now?

149

You ask a good question. *The Shariyat* tells us how a Co-worker with God differs from a Co-worker with the Mahanta.

Chelas of ECK are Co-workers with the Mahanta. The ECK Masters are Co-workers with God because they have returned to the Ocean of Love and Mercy.

Look in the indexes of *The Shariyat,* Books One and Two. The entries *Co-worker* and *Co-worker with SUGMAD* refer to text that will give you a better idea about the steps to perfection.

Spiritual Goal Setting

I am confused about detachment and how it works in terms of striving for anything, or if we even should strive. Should a person try to get ahead or be successful in worldly terms, or should he just put his efforts into spiritual unfoldment (aside from supporting himself and dependents if he has them)? Is wanting, striving, and desiring just another Kal trap?

In the past, too much attention was put on detachment. The wrong definition taken for it was "don't get involved in life." In ECK we are detached, but we are also the great lovers of life. Can it be any other way for a Co-worker with the SUGMAD?

The path of ECKANKAR is only to enhance our spiritual growth. How does this unfoldment come about? Through daily duties. Yes, it is all right to set goals in business. We can set goals, work to accomplish them, and still be working in the arena of detachment. Detachment means that if our plans don't work out as we think they should, life won't crush us.

The path of ECK ought to bring a zest for life. Each activity contains within it the seed of a spiritual lesson. We do not make spiritual progress by doing as little as possible in life. The individual must make an honest evaluation of his talents, interests, and training to decide what goals he wishes to strive for.

Every time he sets out to win small goals, he is aware in Soul consciousness that their only purpose is to give him instruction in becoming a citizen of the spiritual hierarchy.

We must first give to life if we expect life to give anything in return. This is the divine law. Life presents a whole series of opportunities. These let us tap into the God Force for aid. This is achieved through the regular practice of the Spiritual Exercises of ECK.

This past year I had dozens of waking dreams and Golden-tongued Wisdom about a certain goal I thought would manifest at the ECK Worldwide Seminar this year. It didn't happen. How can I become more conscious of my spiritual evolution if I can't trust these dreams and Golden-tongued Wisdom?

For every male and female in ECK, the dream is Mastership. Experiences on the inner planes of having gained Mastership simply point out your potential, for the Vairagi Adepts have put you into the circle of candidates for ECK Mastership. Whether one stays or goes, it is partly a matter of personal choice.

One's selection as a candidate is only the beginning.

After that, the individual must determine to live and act as the ECK Masters do, giving love and service to life in every way imaginable. This second part of the tests for ECK Mastership is what many candidates find very hard, but it is the real key to living and moving in the highest streams of Light and Sound.

I am writing you to get some guidance. As a low-profile type of person, I sometimes have difficulty asserting myself. Sometimes getting ahead seems to mean stepping on others, and I don't want to do this. But I wonder: What's the balance between being active and waiting for what I want to be provided by the ECK?

Many others in ECK have the same problem as you in resolving how to live the life of ECK and not get caught up in power plays over those less able than us.

We are not passive people, content to let people do to us what they will. Soul is a joyful, creative, and active being.

Note the word *creative*. It means that we decide what we want to achieve in our lives, and then we make step-by-step goals to accomplish our ends.

Whatever profession you as an ECKist are in, you will feel an urge toward growth. This is natural for Soul. We do all we can to keep the goodwill of others as we go about gathering our rich spiritual experiences in this life. But we do recognize limits.

Some people take advantage of us. They make us puppets and allow for no growth in our development. In such an event, make careful plans to achieve your goals where you work (further study toward accreditation), or investigate a new place of employment.

You are unhappy where you are. That means you are ready to change your outlook to something broader on how to live ECK.

After the Fifth Initiation

I understand we will know our mission in life once we reach our Fifth Initiation. Is this true? If so, how can we learn more about our mission before we reach this level?

In a broad way, we do learn our mission in life at the Fifth Initiation. Yet some people may forget their mission, so they fail in consciousness. Whether or not they do slide backward, each Fifth Initiate has his or her own state of awareness. In fact, that is true of everyone, regardless of initiation level.

You can learn more about your mission in life during each initiation before the Fifth. However, this is true only of those who do the Spiritual Exercises of ECK with love.

I've been puzzled for years over the difference between success in the spiritual life and that of the physical life. Although I'm a Higher Initiate, my personal life in terms of employment and finances is literally in shambles. You would think that spiritual advances would give some light on my life's work. In some ways, I've put ECK first so much that my job has suffered.

Others have seen themselves in what has happened to you. I have several letters on my desk that ask, "We've got the Sound and Light; now what?" Then go out and earn self-mastery, I would say. But then comes the natural question: How? And so the mind goes.

In the meantime there are the regular problems that used to confront us. If someone caught us in a moment of honesty and asked, "How is your life different from what it was before ECKANKAR?" what could we say? Surely, there must be a way to put into words and practice the benefits of ECK!

Step one: Let's look around and see what surrounds our state of consciousness. Meaning: What are we doing with our time every day, and what are we learning from it, if anything? What do we expect from living? What do we expect after we finish living in this body? If the answer to that comes into focus, then we could

153

say, I know my spiritual mission in life.

Tonight I played Ping-Pong with someone who is better than I am. This is good, for there is always someone better than we are in something. Fortunately he also lives close by and enjoys the game for exercise. There is a need for exercise for the body just as there is a need for the spiritual exercise for Soul.

It's the little things in life, my friend. Our mission is to find our place in the spiritual community and serve God as a carrier of the Light and Sound.

Thinking from the End

What does "thinking from the end" mean as spoken of in the ECK books?

The ancient Greeks were experts in this technique. It means the ability to visualize your desires and give them life by filling them with feeling. Think of a goal, then set intermediate steps leading to it.

To reach the state of God-Realization, put yourself in the ECK Master's shoes. Each time you confront a problem, ask: "What would the Mahanta do in this situation?" Then do it. That's thinking from the end.

The ECK is continually pressing forward for expression through you. Thinking from the end is the creative process that makes life a controllable and enjoyable thing.

How Can You Be a Lover of Life?

How can I live my life less in the grips of power and more in the grace of love?

It is easy to see that those with compassion have learned to love by the trials of suffering, now and in some time past. Coleridge said, "He prayeth best who loveth best/All things both great and small."

A quiet life is all most of us hope for, but the ECK takes a little of us at first, then a little more, until It has all of us.

Two kinds of people are in ECK: those who love the Mahanta above all, and those who love themselves more. The Outer Master is the main channel of the ECK to bring about reactions in chelas, but the tests only unmask the individual for what he is: a lover of God or a servant of power.

With love, I am always with you.

Finding Your Cycle

Please tell me about cycles of activity and rest. When I feel reluctant to get involved in outer activities in ECK, I am not sure what this means.

There are rest points in eternity, and one often finds a cycle of outer activity followed by seeking out quietness. It's a natural part of life, and one must not be too concerned about it.

ECKists work among the public as individuals serving the ECK. One can always be a listening ear as well, as a silent vehicle for Divine Spirit, when the occasion comes. We can serve as vehicles for Spirit by just being ourselves.

Spiritual Success

I have been disappointed in my experiences so far in ECK. I also have felt a great imbalance in my life. Isn't ECK supposed to straighten this out?

The approach to success in spiritual things is like success in high-school sports. Some youths trying out for basketball dribble the ball down the street. They touch, bounce, and toss the basketball until it becomes an extension of themselves.

The same is true of football players. In fact, some coaches make errant players carry the ball around campus the week following an error that lost the game for the team.

It also takes a complete commitment in learning Soul Travel or meeting the Inner Master. This is something nobody can give to you. The motivation must be from within yourself. After you develop the self-discipline to do the Spiritual Exercises of ECK faithfully, then you can look for results.

The same discipline is needed if one wants to become a doctor. A few weeks of halfhearted study does not create an M.D. Years of self-sacrifice are usually the price of success. What does the medical student hope to accomplish that drives him toward his goal? For some it is merely money, but for others it is to make life easier for others living on this planet. But whatever is behind his drive, he has drive.

Your approach to the spiritual exercises can be more flexible and experimental. The guidepost is a monthly report—to yourself, if necessary. Keep a log that lists insights or dreams, or something that happened in contemplation. If your log shows no success within a month, try both a new spiritual exercise as well as a new word taken from one of the ECK books.

There's a definite spiritual current in ECKANKAR. It's like climbing a mountain. Take your time so you can acclimate to the altitude.

Conscious Evolution

Recently I have become interested in subliminal tapes. Is there any spiritual harm to using them? How do they fit in with the goals of Soul?

156

The problem with subliminal tapes is that they bypass the conscious mind. You're letting somebody tinker with your mind without any idea of what is being planted in it without your knowledge.

The people who sell these tapes may have high ethics, but we get into the bad habit of trusting people whose major interest is in selling tapes, rather than in our welfare. Our defenses are let down. The first time some trickster puts a hypnotic suggestion on the tape (e.g., buy another tape), we are trapped.

Subliminal tapes run us toward mechanical evolution. Soul's desire is conscious evolution.

Some of my friends go to a medium. This brought to mind all the spiritual and not-so-spiritual programs available these days. How do they differ from ECK and Soul Travel?

Mediums attract a lot of curiosity seekers, but it's nothing more than spiritual window-shopping. They're making the rounds. If the hoopla changes as often as the monthly TV programming, the medium holds the crowd. Otherwise, the crowd leaves for new hoopla.

This sort of thing is needed for those people who must have the experience of finding a short-haul guru.

Too many think in terms of "Give me God-Realization and true fulfillment will be mine." But hardly a one has thought about what he will do after that great moment comes. One finds that with spiritual liberation comes total freedom and total responsibility.

Who will go to the store on Thursday for the groceries? Will the fix-it man accept divine love in trade for repairing the car's muffler? Somehow, there's a big gap in people's minds about what they are today and what they'll be once they experience the most sacred of occasions in the presence of the SUGMAD.

I don't want to disillusion anybody about the experience of God, but they ought to be somewhat realistic about it when it does come.

Is there any restriction about ECK initiates attending meetings of other groups, such as EST? Although I used to dislike its confrontive policies, I recently find there is nothing in it that contradicts the ECK way.

First of all, don't ever let any other person tell you how to run your universe, including me. You were sincere in wanting to know my advice to ECKists in regard to getting involved with other groups, so I offer it for your consideration.

You alone must make the decision of whether or not to be a member of more than one group at a time. I do however ask that the teachings from other groups be left outside the ECK Satsang class, because two different teachings do not mix. Each discipline emanates from a unique vibrational current, even as each individual has a personal aura.

A person who throws himself wholeheartedly in two directions and still hopes to do either of them justice is simply fooling himself. Problems come up that seem to be from no rightful origin. They arise from the conflict of two distinct paths that each have their own force field. When the two come into proximity of each other, there is a clash in the invisible worlds that works out in the physical world as problems that seem to have no reason for being.

None of these problems are of such a nature that you cannot deal with them, for you are a strong person inside. This should be a personal project for you, however; each individual's circumstances are different.

The general principle is that two paths do not mix if one tries to live both of them to the hilt at the same time. But you can try to blend the two and see what there is for learning. I would rather have people do something and get experience than be sitting on their hands while life passes them by.

Spiritual Goals and Religions

What's the purpose of religions? How do they help Soul reach Its spiritual goals?

Religions have been developed to aid mankind in reaching God. Each religion was and is a channel of ECK to spiritually uplift a certain band of consciousness. However, too often religions get away from their original purpose and begin to manipulate society.

When truth comes into a person or a religion, it makes a passive state active. In this active state, people are driven toward action. Here's the rub: They act from their own imperfect states of consciousness.

One of the most destructive forces unleashed by the pure water of truth is some people's lust for power. They wish to control others. So truth in expression becomes a highly charged accelerator that fires up the engines of karma. As people work off their karma, truth expresses itself through their hard-won spiritual lessons.

To expand that last thought: When truth enters the vessel of a person or a religion, things begin to pop. As far as we're concerned, truth does not operate in a vacuum. Therefore, people who've been touched a little by truth try to express it in their daily lives: within a family structure, a business, or a religion.

A religion is composed of layers and layers of people with different states of consciousness. Some of those individuals act nobly toward others, while a few try to use truth for personal gain. The latter like power politics and cause a lot of problems for others before their karmic engines run out of steam.

ECKANKAR has the same faults within its infrastructure. That's because it too is composed of many different kinds of people. Some are always trying to limit the truth that comes through ECKANKAR. The rest of us do all we can to reopen the channel of truth. A never-ending struggle, but worth the trouble for many people like you.

When Others Leave ECK

I don't know what to make of it when others leave ECK, especially Higher Initiates. Can you explain what happens to their spiritual goals?

Each person on the path of ECK has his choice, his free will. Every attempt is made to shake one's faith in the ECK, but the lover of Divine Spirit always goes to the inner for his own reality. No one can upend the Sound and Light of God.

The Fifth Initiation, says *The Shariyat,* is where the Mahdis "first faces what is known as truth, or the Reality of God. If he fails the tests which must be confronted constantly during his daily life, then he could slip back into the world of the mind." Soul can fall back into the lower regions.

There is a safeguard so this does not happen to us. The key is simply the faithful practice of the Spiritual Exercises of ECK, the Friday fast, writing monthly initiate reports (whether or not they are mailed), and the study of the ECK books and discourses.

We are in for harder times to come. A lot of ECK initiates will look at the picture put in front of them and become stronger in ECK. Others who have no experience with Soul Travel or the Light and Sound will call it all a big delusion and go to another teaching. Quite honestly, truth doesn't fit between the covers of any one book, or even a multivolume set of books. It, like the ECK, encompasses all dimensions of life.

Those who leave because they cannot understand the living teachings of ECK today will nevertheless have gained some benefit from them. Whatever benefit they gain spiritually may someday guide them more directly to the SUGMAD.

In the future, the path of ECK will become broader still. Those who are narrow of mind will not be able to go with that expansion. Yet some ECKists will remain friends with those who leave ECK, because the ECKists' grounding is so strong that no division can shake it.

You do not have to Soul Travel to be successful in
ECK. Another way to God-Realization is to give tender
love and care to every action, because of your love for
the SUGMAD.

11
Soul Travel

I have searched for almost thirteen years to find a path with an inner and outer teacher. I've learned a lot about ECK through books, but I feel frustrated because I'm still not experiencing Soul Travel. I wonder, Is ECK for me?

I can appreciate your hesitation in regard to the teachings of ECK. I had the same uncertainties when I wrote to Paul Twitchell years ago as I looked for a spiritual path.

Soul Travel is one of the foundations of ECKANKAR. It ranges from the unmistakable state of becoming aware of yourself in the Soul body, while traveling on one of the neighboring planes, to more subtle ones, such as having an insight into a concern that previously seemed beyond your abilities to solve.

The dynamic kind of Soul Travel is unforgettable for anyone who is able to have it. It occurs through the practice of the Spiritual Exercises of ECK.

Desire to Soul Travel

What can I do to get colorful, vivid, exciting, and dramatic inner experiences like the ones which some ECK speakers have related?

Those inner experiences you describe are usually Soul Travel. It takes a very strong desire to do it, unless the Mahanta, the Living ECK Master gives you a special hand.

And then, he must give an extraordinary boost, even to those ECK initiates who do their spiritual exercises with love and feeling. People must want to Soul Travel very much, otherwise they won't develop themselves spiritually for the journey. The worlds of ECK can overwhelm people who are not prepared for them.

So how can you get these dramatic inner experiences? Start by doing your spiritual exercises every night before you go to bed. Then, develop methods to remember your dreams better by using a tape recorder or taking notes.

Invent new ways of doing the spiritual exercises given in the ECK discourses. Make them more dramatic and appealing, to fit you personally.

I've been in ECK twenty years, but I've not yet had a conscious out-of-body experience. Is there some kind of blockage within my subconscious? Would subliminal tapes help me?

It's good to be a Hound of Heaven, but not at all costs.

We cannot force ourselves into a Soul Travel experience if that's not the best thing for us. Twenty years of trying is hardly a split second in eternity for Soul, but to us it represents much of our spiritual life.

Try backing off Soul Travel and master the dream state first. The dream state is just another aspect of Soul awareness, so it's the place to set a good foundation for Soul Travel.

Remember to pursue Mastership gently and not push. Instead of pushing to do Soul Travel, back up and learn all you can about the dream state. Both it and Soul Travel are doors to the same spiritual worlds. So experiment with your dreams.

If done right, you'll soon find yourself awake in the other planes without the need for Soul Travel of the popularly imagined kind: A Saturn rocket that blasts you to the stars. Dreams are a gentler, equally effective doorway to spiritual exploration.

Putting Your Experiences into Words

If the higher worlds are without form, why did Paul Twitchell occasionally describe the Soul Plane as having shapes and places?

The Soul Plane and the higher worlds of God do not depend upon form for existence, as do the lower worlds.

Rebazar Tarzs, Paul's guide in *The Tiger's Fang,* arranged it so Paul could record his journey beyond the Mental Plane. Since Paul's mind, like all minds, could not go to the Soul Plane or beyond, Rebazar fashioned images for Paul to remember his experience.

Paul's real contribution in *The Tiger's Fang* is his description of the Sound of God. Today, ECKANKAR teaches the Sound Current, which makes it quite different from the orthodox religions of the world.

165

Simplify Your Experience

What's the purpose of Soul Travel? Is it more important than learning divine love, for example?

I am really more interested in having an individual open up to divine love than to achieve anything else, including Soul Travel. All that Soul Travel is, is one means available for you to find the love of God.

The path of ECK is much broader than Soul Travel, of course. There are many ways that the ECK expresses Itself to the human race, but many of the ways seem so commonplace that the average person doesn't see or hear them anymore.

This includes all the sounds of nature: a gentle breeze, rustling leaves in autumn, the chirping of crickets, the purring of a cat, the low hum of a refrigerator, the laughing of children at play, and hundreds of other examples.

You mentioned your practice of former times where you went off by yourself to commune with God and nature. If you could ever recapture this, you would find much of the spiritual unfoldment you are looking for.

Our society admires more mental things today: food for thought—either in writings or speeches. From this material, the Living ECK Master looks for an avenue to Soul that will result in the human mind stepping aside for a moment, letting the miracle of divine illumination occur.

You do not have to Soul Travel to be successful in ECK. Another way to God-Realization is to give tender love and care to every action, because of your love for the SUGMAD.

A direct and simple way to God is to find someone or something to love every day. Then, at bedtime, let your thoughts gently drift back to this moment of love in your day. Contemplate on that with love and joy. Your contemplative exercises can be as simple as that.

How Do You Use Your Imagination?

I've heard that we should use our imagination to Soul Travel, but can we use too much imagination? Sometimes I'll have an experience and am not sure whether I've made it up.

To imagine Soul Travel is the first thing one must do before actually getting out of the body.

A girl who plays second base for a baseball team in town is called a "natural." But she works hard at her fielding and hitting. Her brothers are all good ball players, and in her mind she imagines herself every bit as good as they are. And so she *is* good, not only because of her imagination, but mainly because she practices harder than the other girls on the team.

Keep on imagining that you do Soul Travel, and one day you will suddenly do it. You will have no more doubt about the difference between imagination and Soul Travel. Wait and see!

Uses of Soul Travel

How and for what purpose were the pyramids constructed?

Your question about the pyramids is a real chance for you to learn Soul Travel.

Soul learns by doing things. Studies show that a person learns faster by doing, rather than by just listening to others. If your question about the pyramids is more than idle curiosity, I'll get you started in your research.

167

The historical starting point for the pyramids goes back to Atlantis, the continent that once included the Bahamas, where you now live. It was an advanced civilization that boasted giant pyramids. They were the inspiration for later replicas in Egypt and Central America.

The Atlanteans had developed science beyond anything known today, including exotic means of space travel for the colonization of nearby planets. The huge continent eventually broke up and sank, but only after many years of cataclysms that left little trace of its former greatness.

During the final series of earthquakes and volcanoes about 12,000 B.C., the Atlanteans packed their goods and fled to Europe, Africa, and the Americas. They took along the culture of their motherland, thus accounting for the similarity of architecture and customs found in widely scattered places like Egypt and Central America, both of which are sites of colossal pyramids.

The pyramids and the smaller monuments built in the same complex were mainly for religious reasons. After the death of the pharaoh, the Egyptians took it for granted that the king would continue with the duties and rituals he had enjoyed as ruler in his earthly life. Therefore, the pyramids held a duplicate of all possessions he had owned on earth, for use in the afterlife.

Viewed from above, the shape of a pyramid suggests a flood of light from heaven shining upon the earth. But if one looks at it from the ground level, the pyramid seems more like a stairway to heaven.

The grandest pyramids were from the golden age of the Old Kingdom of Egypt. The builders still had knowledge of highly advanced Atlantean measuring and cutting methods. This somewhat explains the remarkably close fit of stones in the Great Pyramid. But if we even mentioned antigravity devices as building tools, critics would use that as a blade against ECK doctrines, which care only about showing Soul the way out of this material prison.

Today's archaeologists say that the pyramids were built by slaves, who dragged tons of stone up temporary ramps along the sides of the pyramids. This is certainly true of the later pyramids, which were of a cruder construction than those of the Old Kingdom of about 2500 B.C.

In his talks, the Living ECK Master usually avoids talking about the scientific marvels of Atlantis. He would rather have the ECK chelas go to the inner planes for their own understanding of ancient world history as it really happened.

Here's the way to do that: First, learn all you can about the pyramids from books on Egypt and Atlantis. A strong desire to learn ancient history will tell the Mahanta that you really do want to know about them. Second, take any questions that come up in your research to the Mahanta in contemplation.

To get you started, look for these books in a good library: *Atlantis: The Antediluvian World* by I. Donnelly (New York: Harper, 1949), *The Testimony of the Spade* by Geoffrey Bibby (New York: A. Knopf, 1956), and *The History of Atlantis* by Lewis Spence (Philadelphia: David McKay & Company, 1927).

The reference librarian may be able to help you if the books are not in the card catalog. Or you may visit a book dealer who specializes in finding out-of-print books, since these are old titles.

Saturate yourself with the subject of the pyramids. Take questions to the Inner Master. Chant your word as usual, but ask for answers to come in the best way.

They may come during Soul Travel or in a dream. Or the Master may guide you to a new book.

Research into the past for a study of the pyramids is a wonderful idea because underneath the wealth of history is a pattern of the ancient people who either obeyed or abused the laws of ECK. Their mistakes can benefit you, if you learn to avoid them.

I hope this gets you going in the right direction. Whether or not you do such in-depth research is entirely up to you. Frankly, if it's done leisurely, a study of this sort can be highly enjoyable.

Do Animals Soul Travel?

I would like to know if animals such as lions, cows, and dogs have Soul Travel experiences.

Some animals do. They're the same as people, in that animals have many different levels of consciousness.

Like us, all animals dream. Some remember, many don't. Specially gifted ones, like spiritually advanced people, do Soul Travel. In time, scientific research will be able to expand its knowledge of what happens when people and animals sleep.

ECK initiates can do such research now. They can begin exploring their interests in these fields of knowledge through dreams or Soul Travel. Eventually, science will catch up to the knowledge of those who already can explore the spiritual states of living beings—human or animal—by Soul Travel.

When You Don't Remember

Why am I unconscious of any spiritual or Soul Travel experiences I may be having during contemplation or at other times?

First, I would like to ask, Do you have any recall of either the Light or Sound of ECK? Look in *The Spiritual Notebook* for the different forms the ECK may take in our Spiritual Eye or inner hearing.

Have you had any dream of the Inner Master at any time? Some people don't until several years after they begin the study of ECK. Others would frankly be more comfortable in another study, for there is one provided by God to fit each of us.

What would happen to your emotions if you were to recall a Soul Travel experience before proper preparations were made to build spiritual stamina? It is hard to say.

For instance, a devoted ECKist on the path today wanted to see a past life where she had been a chela of the Living ECK Master of the times. She carried a haunting fear that she had done something terrible to him in that lifetime and that the consequences had come with her into the present time. After months without an answer, the past records opened to show her as a chela of Rebazar Tarzs.

She had gained a high degree of unfoldment then, but one willful act against him—without cause—had thrown her off the path of Light and Sound. She saw the exact violation, which I won't dwell on here. The point of this example is that the truth almost drove her to despair.

Several weeks ago, an impatient chela begged to have his karma speeded up. He wanted to advance rapidly on the path to make up time lost in recent years by squandering pearls of opportunity. He has no idea what is he asking. The path of ECK is only for the Soul that is sincere about returning to God. My only function is to give It assistance in Its own efforts toward that supreme goal.

I won't hold you to the way of ECK if you feel it is not for you. You are not ready for Soul Travel now. It would not be good for you. In *ECKANKAR: Illuminated Way Letters* Paul Twitchell stated: "There are those who cannot see anything in ECK beyond what is known as Soul Travel alone. They limit themselves to the possibility of falling into the psychic trap of Kal Niranjan, the king of the negative power." Look to your dreams for one month, keep a dream notebook, and see what results you get.

I have not met you on the inner recently, or at least I do not remember it. I look forward to being able to recollect my experiences.

Do not be too concerned if your memory of the inner experiences goes more into the background for a while. The ECK Masters work with the individual through the different planes in order to maintain balance in the physical, everyday life.

Look to the Inner Master for spiritual insight. This may come through gentle nudgings on how to try something new with the spiritual exercises. Do those things in your contemplations that you like to do.

It is often very effective to finish contemplation as usual, then, when going to bed for the night, simply ask the Inner Master in everyday language: "I give you permission to take me where I am ready to go. This is in your hands." Go to sleep without another thought of it.

Take your time, and don't hurry. It is better to go slowly and learn the lessons of Divine Spirit well.

Human Reactions

When I Soul Travel, I sometimes wake up feeling physically ill. Why?

This is the reaction of the human consciousness to the infusion of Divine Spirit. It is similar to the reaction that occurs when a wire is stretched across the positive and negative poles of a battery. Spirit will have Its way, and after several months this discomfort will pass.

Beyond Soul Travel

Although I had many Soul Travel experiences when I was young, I am no longer able to Soul Travel or see the inner light. What is the cause of this? I do not understand my spiritual blindness.

It is a great privilege for Soul to incarnate into the physical plane. The lessons of Soul that are gained here cannot be done as well elsewhere.

You have contact with the Sound and Light of ECK. This brings with it an assurance and confidence that allows one to live each moment with fullness of heart.

Just about everyone with any time at all in ECK benefits from the expansion of consciousness, also known as Soul Travel. This may come as an increased awareness and insight into everyday situations, or spiritual understanding. Not always will one experience sensational out-of-body travels.

This is better, because when one reaches the Soul Plane, there is no more Soul Travel.

Soul Travel brings Soul through the lower worlds— the Astral, Causal, Mental, and Etheric planes—until one reaches the Soul Plane. There Soul Travel stops because it is limited to the regions of matter, energy, space, and time. Here, one begins to work with seeing, knowing, and being. It is a whole new ball game.

The veil lifts gradually from our spiritual eyesight as we become ready to look farther into the spiritual

173

realities. The pace is measured so that the chela can maintain his balance while still living in the physical body.

Soul and the Bodies

I recently read about the phenomenon of a physical body changing hands between two Souls, with the new Soul being called a walk-in. *Can you tell me more?*

There are walk-ins for several different reasons, but you can read more about this in books at the library or on the newsstands. Paul Twitchell touched on it briefly in *The Three Masks of Gaba.*

When someone puts too much attention on a negative thing such as walk-ins, he himself could become party to such an intrusion either as victim or perpetrator. This is why I put no emphasis on it in the outer works of ECK.

Can Soul operate more than one physical body at a time on this planet?

Yes, It can. But it is a skill usually reserved for those who have put a great deal of energy into spiritual unfoldment, like the ECK Masters—and sometimes a handful of Higher Initiates.

Some of the old saints could run two or more bodies at once. A case in point is Padre Pio, who gave his whole life in service to God. How many are willing and able to do that?

Can Soul Get Lost?

For many years now I've had a certain fear of traveling in the Far Country. I've heard about the chela and Master being in awesome battles in the other worlds.

174

Not having enormous faith in my own fighting abili-
ties, I wonder what would happen if I lost the battle
and were killed or captured. Do accidents occur while
traveling the Far Country, like being separated from
the Inner Master and getting lost forever?

First, not everyone gets to fight in such inner
battles. Among the more adventurous dream travelers
are those born in January. They may often fight such
battles. But other people, even some born in January,
choose inner experiences that better suit their peace-
ful natures. You are one of these.

No chela is forever separated from the Master
through some accidental mix-up of signals on the inner
planes. The "Far Country" may not be the best description of the nearness of your own inner worlds. You
cannot become lost in them, because the Far Country
is your personal universe.

The Mahanta is simply there to acquaint you with
your own worlds of being.

Can You Overcome Fear of Soul Travel?

When fear stops you from continuing a Soul Travel
experience, can the Mahanta help you overcome that
fear?

First of all, I'm glad to see you using the word
continuing. It means that you have at least had a little
experience with Soul Travel.

You are right, it is only fear that stops us from
progress with Soul Travel. What happens when you
love someone or something with your whole heart?
Right, fear is pushed out of your mind!

Therefore, can you go into contemplation by putting a thought into your heart about something you did

once that made you happier than you'd ever been before? Then take with you the thought: I love the SUGMAD with all that is within me.

This takes practice, of course. A friend of mine had a Soul Travel experience for the first time a few weeks ago. One of the lady ECK Masters told her that she herself had been able to Soul Travel for centuries. A big word of caution from the ECK Master was this: "Trust only the Mahanta and chant your word; he will be near you for protection at all times."

I hope that this will help you get over your fear. It is quite a natural thing, but you will see it growing less powerful as you keep on with the spiritual exercises.

Protection during Soul Travel

I am an African chela able to get out of my body while asleep. Is this Soul Travel, and is it dangerous? Our elders believe this experience comes when an evil force is around and warn that people can die from it.

The experience you describe indeed pertains to awareness in the Soul consciousness. Much of what your elders say about Soul awareness outside the body is true unless one is an ECKist under the spiritual guidance and protection of the Mahanta.

The Inner Master will often give the acolyte the experience of Soul Travel. The reason for this is to give assurance of Soul's survival outside of the body.

Once this lesson has been learned, it is not at all unusual for similar events to pass out of the initiate's remembrance as the Master leads one farther into the God Worlds of ECK.

Eventually the ECKist learns to follow the Law of Silence in regard to his inner life, for his experiences can upset the uninitiated. Most people live in great fear of the mysteries of life and try to prevent those who are adventurous in Spirit from looking beyond the realities of everyday existence.

Your spiritual life is in the hands of the Mahanta, the Inner Master, who alone can lead you to the greater Light and Sound of ECK.

Belief in Your Experiences

How can you tell the difference between an out-of-body experience and a very vivid dream?

When it happens, you'll know. You won't need to ask anyone to verify a Soul Travel experience, because it is literally out of this world.

A word of caution, however, should you have one. Be most careful with whom you share it. You are the genuine authority on that experience. Unless the person you confide in has Soul traveled, he or she may dismiss your experience as only a vivid dream.

Don't let anyone make you doubt your spiritual experiences.

When You Pass On

Why do some ECKists Soul Travel more often than others? I would like to learn to Soul Travel in order to be prepared when I die. I am a little afraid of it now and would like it to be a joyful experience, since I am quite old and may be passing soon.

The ECK works in Its own way with each of us. It will bring whatever is right for our spiritual progress.

Some initiates never have Soul traveled nor seen a particular manifestation of Divine Spirit, such as the Blue Light. We are all different.

It is of singular importance for us to contact the

Mahanta, the Inner Master. Depending upon our station in life, we may become aware of either Light, Sound, or the appearance of the Inner Master. These are inward expressions.

Other valid signs of the ECK reported by other initiates of ECK include a knowingness during the waking life of divine intervention. Otherwise it can be an impression of help from a mysterious source that one immediately accepts as the Holy Spirit.

It is not good if someone has too many striking inner experiences, because all they may do is put him out of step with his friends and family. The secret of ECK is to live in step with all of life if that is possible.

The moment of translation can be a wonderful experience, the highlight of Soul's chapter on earth. There is nothing special that one has to do as an ECKist to prepare outwardly for the event. Make the usual arrangements for the disposal of the physical remains. Leave it in the hands of the doctor to decide when the body is no longer suitable as a house for Soul.

I will be with you at the moment chosen for this occasion. This is usually a pleasant and spiritually invigorating event in one's life. As one enters into it, there come the memories of having done it before. All fear and doubt vanish. The radiant form of the Mahanta appears to take the individual to the worlds of light and love of the Soul Plane.

The ECK Masters are usually so down-to-earth and matter-of-fact that people immediately feel comfortable with them, as they would with an old friend.

12

The ECK Masters

*H*ow can I tell if the ECK Masters are real? I am new to ECKANKAR.

Once anyone has met Rebazar Tarzs physically or on the inner planes, there is no further question that he is a real being.

But not everyone has earned the privilege.

It is interesting to note that when one first steps onto the path of ECK, he may have a number of experiences that give proof of Soul's existence beyond death. He is also shown the reality of the ECK Masters of the Order of the Vairagi.

Then, over the years, he unfolds. Sometimes he does so without recognition of his expanded state of consciousness.

His inner and outer experiences reach a new level, but his awareness of this is nonexistent until a radical change occurs on the physical plane, like the selection of a new Living ECK Master. This jars him in the awakened state, and what he discovers is often unsettling.

His experiences have toned down and interwoven

themselves into his everyday life. Without understanding the ways of Divine Spirit that grow increasingly more subtle, he looks outwardly and asks: "Is ECKANKAR still the Life Force it was when I first stepped on the path?" Of course—and more so than before.

Inner and Outer Master

I've been a little scared of meeting the Outer Master. I'm afraid I will do something stupid in front of you and fail an important test.

The ECK Masters will not embarrass anyone who really wants to reach God-Realization. They well remember their own trials as they struggled to reach the mountain of God.

They are usually so down-to-earth and matter-of-fact that people immediately feel comfortable with them, as they would with an old friend.

Who and what is the Mahanta? Is it anything like the waves of consciousness I experience in my contemplations?

Very few understand about the various levels of consciousness, as you do. People must come to their own conclusions about what and who the Mahanta is, and how this relates to spiritual realization. All the Mahanta wants is to lead the individual to perfection, such as it might be.

How can you be with all chelas at once?

In his physical body, the Mahanta, the Living ECK Master is like everyone else and can only be in one place at a time.

In the Soul body, however, he is like the air that you breathe. He is everywhere. As the ECK, he can easily be with you and thousands of others in the very same moment.

To put it another way, you can think of the Mahanta as a body and yourself as one tiny cell within his body. Millions of other cells are in it, too. The Mahanta is always with all the cells within his body, whether they are in his toe or in his head.

What exactly is the Living ECK Master's real job?

It is simply to help Soul find Its way home to God.

The idea is simple, but carrying it out is something else. What makes it hard is that people forget what they're in ECK for. After a few years, they get too used to the ECK teachings to enjoy living the principles.

It's like a child who knows what the parent is going to say before a word is spoken, because the child has known the parent all his life. Finally, he doesn't hear anything that is said anymore.

The Living ECK Master is here to remind the initiate of the spiritual exercises, the three different kinds of fasts, and the monthly initiate reports. Many help him with this mission, and the chelas who realize they are channels for the Mahanta are among those.

I'm not a very emotional person, but every time I see a picture of you or read certain things about you, I cry. Why is this?

It is Soul recognizing the Mahanta. This makes Soul happy. Out here, it explains why you cry.

I've noticed you do very little to sway others toward your ideas or even the ECK teachings. What is the spiritual reason for this?

183

People expect a lot of flashy speeches, but the Living ECK Master purposely keeps things on an even keel. It is all too easy to sway people's emotions with the right words so they make a decision to follow ECK against their will.

It's a spiritual crime to do such a thing.

A part of the seeker's test is seeing beyond the outer personality of the Master. ECK is for the simple and pure of heart, for truth does not make a whole lot of sense to the intellectuals of society.

Why Do the ECK Masters Serve?

What is the secret of becoming a Master? Why do it at all?

Someone once had an interview with a number of ECK Masters. She wanted to know why they served the SUGMAD, the ECK, and the Mahanta. All of them began their reply with: "Because I like to . . . "

In addition, she learned that each did what he could do best. This was the secret of their Mastership and service to God.

Only One Mahanta

Are there Mahantas in other galaxies?

There is only one Mahanta who serves the SUGMAD at a time. But you are right—the Living ECK Master takes a different body for each planet and universe. But the consciousness is one and the same, that of the Mahanta.

Some of the High Initiates recall running several bodies in different places at the same time. That is one of the extraordinary talents of those who serve the SUGMAD.

If you follow the ECK line of development, you could also, one day, be asked by the Order of the Vairagi to work with such talents. It is an exciting mission to be a Co-worker with God.

Blue Star

Why is the Mahanta's light blue? Has it always been blue?

Most people who are ready to meet the Mahanta, the Living ECK Master have evolved spiritually to the Mental Plane. The color of that plane is blue. It is the point at which all the lower forces of an individual must gather and be purified in preparation for his entering the Soul Plane.

The Mahanta is the ECK, and the totality of the Light that emanates from him is the whitest of whites. But like a prism, the density of the Mental Plane is such that blue is the color most often seen there (but not exclusively).

This arrangement of the blue color for the Mahanta has been noted from the beginning of Soul's entrance into the lower worlds.

Why does the Living ECK Master always dress in blue?

Years ago I started to get gentle nudges from the ECK to let other people know about the wonderful teachings of ECK that had brought so much joy to me. But I was scared.

Peddar Zaskq came to me one night in contemplation and asked me the same question that you asked. I learned then that wearing blue clothes is not for everyone, because it would be a dull world if we all wore the same color of clothing.

185

But at certain times when as a chela I was to do something for ECK and my knees would hardly stop shaking, I found that the blue clothes reminded me of the Blue Light of the Mahanta. The blue color gave me courage. It helped me to know that a globe of blue light was always cast around me for protection from any little fears that were trying to hold me back from the Ocean of Love and Mercy.

Later, I just got into the habit of wearing blue, and now I like it. My blue clothes are a reminder to ECK chelas of the Blue Light of the Mahanta.

Presence of the Master

How is the presence of the Mahanta most directly experienced?

You can know the Mahanta's presence most directly by a feeling of warmth and love in your heart.

Some initiates see the Blue Light. Others find the image of the Mahanta in their Spiritual Eye or hear the Sound Current. In whatever way you sense him, he is always with you.

Three Aspects of God

What is the difference between the Mahanta, SUGMAD, and the Master? (I know what a chela is—me.)

Yours is quite a question! I'll try to explain it as simply as possible.

The SUGMAD is our name for God. The SUGMAD, the ECK, and the Mahanta are all three of the same reality.

The SUGMAD has three aspects, and they are also the three bodies of the Mahanta. First is the eternal

186

Mahanta that always lives in the Ocean of Love and Mercy. Second is the ECK. Third is the historical Mahanta, the Living ECK Master. He is the Master, the Godman. People can see and talk with him. The chela who answers the Master's call is taken home to God and becomes a Co-worker with God.

Friends

Do ECK Masters have friends?

They do. The ECK Masters look for pockets of individuals who love the SUGMAD, the ECK, and the Mahanta above all else. They want balanced people who love their families and close ones, and who enjoy the gift of life.

The ECK Masters encourage this small band of truth lovers to carry out a certain mission. Each person in the group is tested often to see how he handles change while serving God. He must embrace the highest ideals of ECK, have a sense of humor, and show good judgment in carrying out his assignments.

The Master in charge does not expect him to know it all, but the individual is to use initiative. He must have the good sense to ask again if he is not clear on a directive.

You will find the ECK Masters to be patient and understanding in nearly every instance. They want you to become an ever-better channel for ECK. It is a privilege to be in their company. But often they are in disguise, and their identities are unsuspected until after they leave.

Yes, ECK Masters have other friends too. Three neighborhood cats come by to see how I'm doing. They are the Hunter (a sleek orange-and-white cat), Sunshine (a fat, out-of-condition cat like Garfield), and

Nubby (black as the darkest night). They are good company, since they don't have strong opinions about trivial matters.

Does the Outer Master have an Inner Master? The chela can talk to the Inner Master, but who do you talk to?

My wife! Seriously, though, when one reaches ECK Mastership, he is responsible to the SUGMAD. The Master's direction is always a result of an ongoing communication with the SUGMAD.

At first, I found it unsettling not to lean upon an Inner Master, because my spiritual position now had me in that role. But that's the point of Mastership, having the spiritual strength to lean upon the Unchangeable. This means doing what must be done in the name of the SUGMAD, confident that no other course of action would answer as well.

It is an exciting position to be in, but it could be terrifying if a Soul did not have Its full spiritual training and were pushed into the role of ECK Master before Its time.

A Continuous Line of Masters

ECKANKAR says there has been a continuous line of ECK Masters for six million years on earth. Now we have the 973rd Living ECK Master. This means that each ECK Master would have had to live an average of six thousand years. Can you please tell me where I have gone wrong in my calculations, or how this could be?

The "973" refers to those who were known as both Mahanta and Living ECK Master. Many Living ECK Masters may serve the interval between each appearance of a Mahanta, the Living ECK Master.

Rebazar Tarzs was a Mahanta, the Living ECK Master. After his spiritual term, he aided those Living ECK Masters who served between himself and Paul Twitchell. If a Living ECK Master translated before his successor was ready, as with Sudar Singh, Rebazar took the Rod of ECK Power in the meantime.

In this connection, *The Shariyat* says that only one Mahanta, the Living ECK Master appears every five to a thousand years. This is a metaphor. It simply means that a new one may come almost immediately or not for a long time.

The image is of the phoenix, a mythical Arabian bird. There was only one of its kind. After five hundred to fifteen hundred years or so, it consumed itself by fire, only to rise again to begin a new cycle.

In a similar way, each new Mahanta, the Living ECK Master comes to bring a new level of spiritual awareness.

Why do some people have such trouble with a change in Living ECK Masters?

Somehow we imagine that when the tests of ECK come to us we will triumph. In our minds we make the tests out to be a simple exercise of some sort that suits our fancy. However, when the test comes from an unexpected and unpleasant quarter, we are upset that someone dirtied the whole picture with a situation that seems so wrong and unspiritual.

Of course, that is the nature of the testing that is brought to the seeker by the Life Force, the ECK Itself. We are always caught looking in the other direction. What matters is how we respond to the onslaught against our imaginations and illusions about what truth is or isn't.

Past Living ECK Masters encountered the same resistance from their chelas. When it came time for them to give up their addiction to small precepts of living, these people turned away from ECK in sorrow, only to wander through the ages with a broken heart. The disillusionments of their insignificance outside of the realm of ECK became a burden too great to carry.

The separation from the hierarchy was of their own making. And by their own efforts did they have to find their way back to the Sound Current. The ECK Masters always stood near them, but spiritual blindness is an all-encompassing thing. It hides all the blessings of the Most High, even when they are within arm's reach.

Even in Paul Twitchell's time, the ECK kept bringing about changes in the works of ECK through Its vehicle, the Living ECK Master. Then, as now, some of us found it difficult to accept changes that would be considered insignificant today.

For instance, many chelas had quite a reaction when he changed his letterhead from "Paul Twitchell" to "ECKANKAR." He switched attention away from the personality of the Living ECK Master in order to reach more Souls ready to step onto the path of ECK.

Some people were not able to stomach misspellings that the printer allowed to creep into the books. But all Paul ever tried to do was lead Soul, by Its own path, back to God.

The true works are on the inner planes, and the key to the works of ECK lies in the faithful practice of the Spiritual Exercises of ECK. We use our creative imagination to take discipline and responsibility for our own lives.

Thus we become Co-workers with God, working at that task of our choice.

The Spiritual Hierarchy

Who are the Bourchakoun? Are they different from the Vairagi Adepts?

Bourchakoun is another name for the Vairagi Adepts. Holy men in India know them as the Eagle-eyed Adepts.

Once an individual becomes a Vairagi Adept, he exists spiritually on the Sound and Light of God. It is his food. And if in a physical body, instead of a supraphysical one, he will, of course, eat food for energy.

How is the hierarchy of Vairagi Adepts run?

The spiritual hierarchy is the foremost example of people who must work together in goodwill and harmony. They make good use of the efforts of many who come together to accomplish a common goal.

The Order of Vairagi Adepts have a chief executive, who is the Living ECK Master. He is surrounded by a board of inner-plane directors who are ECK Masters, specialists in some field or another.

This hierarchy is built upon the idea of the planes that descend from the Ocean of Love and Mercy. There is a designated ruler on each plane, and through him comes the full power of the ECK from above.

Who are the Council of Nine? How can we work with them?

The Council of Nine are the ECK Masters responsible for the distribution of the ECK message in the lower worlds.

If spreading the teachings of ECK is your goal, then put attention upon these timeless ones during contemplation. Lay whatever problem you have on the line, and invite their help. Ask them to accompany you to work or ECK meetings.

Remember, no ECK Master will interfere with your plans unless given an express invitation. So you have to approach them during contemplation to request help formulating plans. Then be aware of them throughout your day.

This team of nine is unbeatable. Like the Sacketts of Louis L'Amour westerns, the brotherhood of ECK Adepts come from all spiritual regions to give help in the work of the SUGMAD.

How Is the Mahanta Chosen?

How were you chosen to be the Mahanta?

My training began several lives ago. In this life, I was put into the stern training of strict schooling as a youth, to prepare me for my mission in this cycle of time.

A number of people are being tested all the time to become members of the Vairagi Order, which they must be before they are next in line for the Mahantaship. But first, they have to go through all the ECK initiations leading up to that level. One who is to become the Mahanta is told of his chosen role when he is an adult, but then years of silence may follow as he goes through even stricter training.

All this is necessary for him to overcome the heavy resistance that he will meet from the Kal Niranjan later in his duties as the spiritual leader. The SUGMAD appoints the Mahanta, and his predecessor announces him to the world.

Where is the Rod of ECK Power kept?

The Rod of ECK Power is the spiritual scepter of the Living ECK Master. It is not an object that can be seen or handled. We know it rather as the power of ECK that comes through the Living ECK Master in order to sustain the creations of God.

The Rod of Power is a concentration of Sound and Light. It is wherever the Master is, for It works through him, and they are inseparable.

Sometimes the Rod of ECK Power is seen as a column of bright white light around the Master. As long as he holds the Rod of Power, he is the agent of the SUGMAD in all ITS worlds.

Who Are the ECK Masters?

Was Saint Paul an ECK Master? Was he responsible for spreading Christianity? Who taught ECK before the Christian era?

The ECK Masters are agents of God whose only concern is to bring spiritual upliftment to each individual who is ready for it. At times this mission has been very difficult.

About three thousand years before the Christian era, ECKANKAR was taught openly in Egypt by Gopal Das. Severe persecution by the followers of the main religion, as well as by proponents of astrology, forced the Nine Unknown ECK Masters to submerge the teachings.

For almost five thousand years since then, the ECK Masters have worked quietly in the background, bringing spiritual upliftment in whatever way possible, even though not as direct as ECKANKAR.

Thus Saint Paul carried forth the basic teachings that later became the body of knowledge called Christianity.

Why do some ECK Masters wear a letter of the alphabet on their Spiritual Eye?

The letter of the alphabet, when it appears on the forehead of an ECK Master, is meant to imprint on the chela's mind. Several ECK Masters who have such a letter visible on their Third Eye are mentioned in *The Secret Way* discourses.

This letter can be used in a three-part spiritual exercise. First, chant your word or HU in contemplation. Second, look at the letter that appears on the ECK Master's Spiritual Eye, and now chant the name of that letter. Third, while still chanting the letter of the alphabet, look directly into the eyes of the ECK Master before you.

This exercise is good for those of you who want to have a close spiritual relationship with a certain ECK Master on the inner planes.

By the way, the final step of this technique will come to you later in contemplation.

What role did the ECK Master Zadok play? Was his mission like Jesus'?

Zadok had a broader mission than did Jesus. This can be a difficult thing to understand, but it is true. Jesus carried the Light of the Word to the people of his times. He tried to give them a little upliftment from the poverty and illness that was so rampant during those times.

He gave himself totally to this purpose, and during the course of his ministering, he met the Living ECK

194

Master, Zadok. Even today, scholars find vague references to this man who figured so prominently in the secret teachings of those connected with the Essenes.

Yet he was not an Essene. As a member of the Vairagi ECK Masters his mission was to be a Wayshower for Soul to find Its way back to God again. Jesus also could take people into heaven, but only to the third heaven. This plane was spoken of by Saint Paul years later.

Is Kata Daki the only female ECK Master? Could you please name some others?

She and Simha, the Lady of ECK, are the only two women known in the outer ECK writings.

Most ECK Masters, male and female, choose to live and work behind the scenes. Other Vairagi Adepts of both sexes exist on earth and the higher planes. The ECK works will reveal the names of others later.

Whether man or woman, all ECK Masters cause a deep love for SUGMAD to awaken in the seeker. This divine love starts many people on the journey home to God.

I know that there are ECK Masters who are Caucasian, Chinese, Indian, and Tibetan. I was wondering if there are any black ECK Masters.

There are many ECK Masters of every race. The foremost black ECK Master known in the ECK writings is Towart Managi. He was the Mahanta, the Living ECK Master in Abyssinia, an ancient kingdom in what is now Ethiopia.

Today, he is the ECK Master in charge of the Shariyat-Ki-Sugmad on the Mental Plane.

Men and women of all races belong to the Order of Vairagi. The SUGMAD makes no distinctions

195

between age, race, sex, or creed. Neither does the Mahanta, the Living ECK Master. He serves all people with complete love.

Was there an ECK Master who lived among the Native Americans of the North American plains? If so, could you please tell me something about him? The Native Americans interest me very much.

Vardrup was the Living ECK Master in the sixteenth century. Originally from Germany, he later sailed to the Americas during Spain's conquest of Mexico. Other Living ECK Masters came to the Americas before and after him, but always in the Soul body.

About 33,000 B.C., the Living ECK Master of the time traveled to the Americas in the Soul body. This was Mksha, whose physical area of service was the Indus Valley. At that time, American natives were hunting the giant sloth, the woolly mammoth, and the giant beaver with spears.

Native Americans of twelve thousand years ago were the Sandia and the Clovis people. They hunted with spears powered by a hand-launching device called an *atlatl* (OT-lottle).

Gopal Das, the Living ECK Master who lived in Egypt about 3000 B.C., traveled via Soul body to teach chelas in North and South America. They lived throughout what is today Canada, Pennsylvania, Nebraska, Montana, California, Mexico, and on down to South America and Cape Horn.

Among the many tribes to spring from these early inhabitants were the Iroquois, Delaware, Cherokee, Fox, Dakota (or Sioux), Apache, Ute, Comanche, Ojibwa, and the Eskimo. The Living ECK Master of the times instructed them in the ancient truths of SUGMAD. He continues to guide all who are ready today.

Master Compilers

I assume the personal dialogues in the ECK works were recorded practically word for word. How do the Masters have such precise recall?

Paul Twitchell wasn't an ECK Master yet when he had the experiences recorded in several of the ECK works.

In general, however, the ECK Masters often speak to one with a highly compact form of communication, much like telepathy. It is like a computer program that compresses a document file for storage.

The chela must decompress the file. He tries to keep the intent of the discourse as he converts it into everyday language. There is no word-for-word utility program that will exactly translate an inner conversation into outer words.

It is even harder than trying to keep the exact meaning of a message in English that is translated into French, then from French into Spanish, and finally from Spanish back into English. The several stages of translation can easily jumble the original message by the time it finishes the loop.

Journey to Mastership

Sometimes I think it would be lonely to have total awareness—all alone, learning but never reaching an end, a home.

There are days when I long to be rid of the lower worlds, but other times I am not sure that I would be happy. If you don't mind, would you please tell me when you reached the point in your life where you knew for sure that you wanted to continue learning into infinity and why. Also, what would one's goals be once he gained total awareness?

Actually, the Mahanta saw my deep desire for truth. He led me step-by-step because of my willingness to follow him. This led eventually to an experience told in *Child in the Wilderness.*

It was on a bridge, with a stranger, that the limitations of my lower self were torn away. I felt alone, exposed, and afraid. And this was during the experience of God-Realization! Also in my book I treat some of the misconceptions that people carry about God Consciousness.

My goal now is simply to serve the SUGMAD. There is nothing else to do. Service to IT is life; anything less is nothing.

Since Paul Twitchell brought ECKANKAR to the public, has anyone besides a Living ECK Master achieved Mastership and been accepted into the Order of Vairagi? Is Mastership really an attainable goal?

Yes, one can become an ECK Master in this life. Levels of ECK Mastership exist, and a few in ECK are near the early levels of it now.

Yet many people don't know what ECK Masters do or how they work. Mostly they work behind the scenes, for, unlike most people, they feel no need to prove anything to others about their states of consciousness.

When a Higher Initiate does become a new ECK Master, it is doubtful that anyone around him will ever know. The ECK Masters are humble. They neither seek nor need the praise of others.

The Living ECK Master speaks for the Vairagi Order. So his mission is a public one: to carry the ECK message to the people of the world.

What are the stages of growth in the higher spiritual levels? What's the relationship between the Master and chela when the chela gets closer to Mastership?

By the time one becomes a Higher Initiate, most of the communication between the Living ECK Master and chela is done through the inner channels.

One of the stages that we come to is learning to work in harmony with all life. This sounds too pat, too flat. But when we can see the Mahanta in all we meet—can see the Light of ECK in the eyes of people passing us in the street—then we can only give love in return to all life.

To qualify for the Order of the Vairagi, Soul must know discrimination in Its love. Warm love for our dear ones, charity (detached love) for the rest of creation.

No one has the capacity to love all life without injury to himself. That is the purpose of discrimination. The ECK Masters practice detachment, but this does not mean lack of compassion. Nor does this mean interfering in somebody else's affairs.

Perhaps the hardest part of my duties is picking up a letter from my desk where someone asks relief from a crushing weight of karma and I know that it must be worked through. There is no shortcut available to him.

Of all those who work in the spiritual field, some are able to move quietly and cooperatively among people, while others generate a storm of controversy and disruption wherever they go. Why is that, all Souls being equal as the spark of God? There is always more to learn about acting as a vehicle for Divine Spirit—what it means and how it's done.

The ECK Masters work strictly through the spiritual hierarchy. That is step number one. They are not in competition with each other. They know their common mission is to serve the great SUGMAD. Secondly, they do so in harmony, nurturing the plus factor, the building element in all they do.

Tests of the Masters

Sometimes the tests in my life get so hard that I wonder if I'll ever make it to Mastership. Did the ECK Masters really have to go through things like this?

Life requires that Soul have every experience. No thought or deed is ever lost—but all is recorded in the Book of Life. Thus Soul learns to have compassion and charity, and to give service to other beings.

The spiritual giants like Rebazar Tarzs have suffered the edge of the sword that wounded the heart, leaving them to cry in despair to God to give them a reason for their anguish.

The greater our consciousness, the more deeply we feel the slights of neglect, lack of consideration, and abuse by people who use our good nature against us. But there is a turning point where the Wheel of Fire, which is slavery to karmic destiny, loses its power over us. Henceforth we emerge from the fog of unknowing and travel freely in the sparkling lands of ECK.

The Masters in ECK are in a state of vairag, or detachment. It is a state of consciousness that is won the hard way, but when the trials are done and Soul is aware of Its relationship with the SUGMAD, then immense love and compassion are the reward.

You cry with the grieving in their sorrow, laugh with the joyous in heart, sit in silence to listen to the heart of someone who has touched the hem of the Lord. You are an inspiration to the weak, a solace for the broken in spirit. Thus you are a saint, a shining light to all who enter your circle of influence.

200

Glossary

Words set in SMALL CAPS are defined elsewhere in this glossary.

ARAHATA. An experienced and qualified teacher for ECKANKAR classes.

CHELA. A spiritual student.

ECK. The Life Force, the Holy Spirit, or Audible Life Current which sustains all life.

ECKANKAR. Religion of the Light and Sound of God. Also known as the Ancient Science of SOUL TRAVEL. A truly spiritual religion for the individual in modern times, known as the secret path to God via dreams and SOUL TRAVEL. The teachings provide a framework for anyone to explore their own spiritual experiences. Established by Paul Twitchell, the modern-day founder, in 1965.

ECK MASTERS. Spiritual Masters who can assist and protect people in their spiritual studies and travels. The ECK Masters are from a long line of God-Realized SOULS who know the responsibility that goes with spiritual freedom.

HU. The secret name for God. The singing of the word HU, pronounced like the word *hue,* is considered a love song to God. It is sung in the ECK Worship Service.

INITIATION. Earned by the ECK member through spiritual unfoldment and service to God. The initiation is a private ceremony in which the individual is linked to the Sound and Light of God.

LIVING ECK MASTER. The title of the spiritual leader of ECKANKAR. His duty is to lead SOULS back to God. The Living ECK Master can assist spiritual students physically as the

201

Outer Master, in the dream state as the Dream Master, and in the spiritual worlds as the Inner Master. Sri Harold Klemp became the Living ECK Master in 1981.

MAHANTA. A title to describe the highest state of God Consciousness on earth, often embodied in the LIVING ECK MASTER. He is the Living Word.

PLANES. The levels of heaven, such as the Astral, Causal, Mental, Etheric, and Soul planes.

SATSANG. A class in which students of ECK study a monthly lesson from ECKANKAR.

THE SHARIYAT-KI-SUGMAD. The sacred scriptures of ECKANKAR. The scriptures are comprised of twelve volumes in the spiritual worlds. The first two were transcribed from the inner PLANES by Paul Twitchell, modern-day founder of ECKANKAR.

SOUL. The True Self. The inner, most sacred part of each person. Soul exists before birth and lives on after the death of the physical body. As a spark of God, Soul can see, know, and perceive all things. It is the creative center of Its own world.

SOUL TRAVEL. The expansion of consciousness. The ability of SOUL to transcend the physical body and travel into the spiritual worlds of God. Soul Travel is taught only by the LIVING ECK MASTER. It helps people unfold spiritually and can provide proof of the existence of God and life after death.

SOUND AND LIGHT OF ECK. The Holy Spirit. The two aspects through which God appears in the lower worlds. People can experience them by looking and listening within themselves and through SOUL TRAVEL.

SPIRITUAL EXERCISES OF ECK. The daily practice of certain techniques to get us in touch with the Light and Sound of God.

SUGMAD. A sacred name for God. SUGMAD is neither masculine nor feminine; IT is the source of all life.

WAH Z. The spiritual name of Sri Harold Klemp. It means the Secret Doctrine. It is his name in the spiritual worlds.

How to Learn More about ECKANKAR
Religion of the Light and Sound of God

Why are you as important to God as any famous head of state, priest, minister, or saint that ever lived?

- Do you know God's purpose in your life?
- Why does God's Will seem so unpredictable?
- Why do you talk to God, but practice no one religion?

ECKANKAR can show you why special attention from God is neither random nor reserved for the few known saints. But it is for every individual. It is for anyone who opens himself to Divine Spirit, the Light and Sound of God.

People want to know the secrets of life and death. In response to this need Sri Harold Klemp, today's spiritual leader of ECKANKAR, and Paul Twitchell, its modern-day founder, have written a series of monthly discourses that give specialized Spiritual Exercises of ECK. They can lead Soul in a direct way to God.

Those who wish to study ECKANKAR can receive these special monthly discourses which give clear, simple instructions for these spiritual exercises.

Membership in ECKANKAR Includes

1. The opportunity to gain wisdom, charity, and spiritual freedom.
2. Twelve monthly discourses which include information on Soul, the spiritual meaning of dreams, Soul Travel techniques, and ways to establish a personal relationship with Divine Spirit. You may study them alone at home or in a class with others.
3. The *Mystic World,* a quarterly newsletter with a Wisdom Note and articles by the Living ECK Master. In it are also letters and articles from members of ECKANKAR around the world.
4. Special mailings to keep you informed of upcoming ECKANKAR seminars and activities worldwide, new study materials available from ECKANKAR, and more.
5. The opportunity to attend ECK Satsang classes and book discussions with others in your community.
6. Initiation eligibility.
7. Attendance at certain meetings for members of ECKANKAR at ECK seminars.

How to Find Out More

To request membership in ECKANKAR using your credit card (or for a free booklet on membership) call (612) 544-0066, weekdays, between 8:00 a.m. and 5:00 p.m., central time. Or write to: ECKANKAR, Att: Information, P.O. Box 27300, Minneapolis, MN 55427 U.S.A.

Introductory Books on ECKANKAR

The Dream Master
Mahanta Transcripts, Book 8
Harold Klemp

If you don't believe dreams are important, you're missing out on more than half your life. Harold Klemp, the Dream Master, can show you how to become more aware of your dreams so you can enjoy a better life. But *The Dream Master* is not just about dreams. It gives you the keys to spiritual survival, and is about living life to the fullest on your way home to God.

Earth to God, Come In Please . . .

Stories from ordinary people who have become aware of a greater force operating in their lives. Their experiences outside the commonplace brought lessons in love and spiritual freedom that changed them deeply. They show how we can make contact with the Voice of God, for spiritual knowledge and awareness beyond words.

ECKANKAR—Ancient Wisdom for Today

Are you one of the millions who have heard God speak to you through a profound spiritual experience? This introductory book will show you how dreams, Soul Travel, and experiences with past lives are ways God speaks to you. You can begin to recognize yourself as a spiritual being.

HU: A Love Song to God
Audiocassette

Learn how to sing an ancient name for God, HU (pronounced like the word *hue*). A wonderful introduction to ECKANKAR, this two-tape set is designed to help listeners of any religious or philosophical background benefit from the gifts of the Holy Spirit. It includes an explanation of the HU, stories about how Divine Spirit works in daily life, and exercises to uplift you spiritually.

For fastest service, phone (612) 544-0066 weekdays between 8:00 a.m. and 5:00 p.m., central time, to request books using your credit card, or look under **ECKANKAR** in your phone book for an ECKANKAR Center near you. Or write: **ECKANKAR, Att: Information, P.O. Box 27300, Minneapolis, MN 55427 U.S.A.**

There May Be an
ECKANKAR Study Group near You

ECKANKAR offers a variety of local and international activities for the spiritual seeker. With hundreds of study groups worldwide, ECKANKAR is near you! Many areas have ECKANKAR Centers where you can browse through the books in a quiet, unpressured environment, talk with others who share an interest in this ancient teaching, and attend beginning discussion classes on how to gain the attributes of Soul: wisdom, power, love, and freedom.

Around the world, ECKANKAR study groups offer special one-day or weekend seminars on the basic teachings of ECKANKAR. Check your phone book under **ECKANKAR**, or call **(612) 544-0066** for membership information and the location of the ECKANKAR Center or study group nearest you. Or write **ECKANKAR, Att: Information, P.O. Box 27300, Minneapolis, MN 55427 U.S.A.**

☐ Please send me information on the nearest ECKANKAR discussion or study group in my area.

☐ Please send me more information about membership in ECKANKAR, which includes a twelve-month spiritual study.

Please type or print clearly   940

Name _____

Street _____ Apt. # _____

City _____ State/Prov. _____

ZIP/Postal Code _____ Country _____